Aliza Barak-Ressler

CRY LITTLE GIRL

The publication of this book was made possible through
the generous support of Samy and Dalia Sheero and
their children, Ezy, Jacky, Yoel and Haviva

Caracas, Venezuela

La edición de este libro ha sido possible gracias a la generosa
colaboración de Samy y Dalia Sheero junto a sus queridos hijos
Ezy, Jacky, Yoel y Haviva

Caracas, Venezuela

Aliza Barak-Ressler

CRY LITTLE GIRL

A Tale Slovakia

Yad Vashem • Jerusalem • 2003

Translated from the Hebrew by Ralph Mandel
Language Editor: Anne Pace
Production Editor: Avital Saf

First printing 2003
Second printing 2009

ISBN 965-308-164-0

Typesetting: Shulamit Yerushalmi, Jerusalem
Printed in Israel, 2003
by Printiv, Jerusalem

Dedicated to my parents, Zippora and Moshe Ressler,
of blessed memory, whose resourcefulness
and courage enabled us to escape danger and death,
against all odds

Contents

Acknowledgments

I want to express my love and gratitude to my devoted husband, Avigdor, for being a bastion of strength and support when I wrote these memoirs, for his encouragement when my spirit flagged and I was on the verge of giving up the project, and for his practical suggestions at times of indecision.

With love to my granddaughter, Omer, who urged me to tell the story and prompted me to write the book.

With thanks to Dr. Gila Fatran, a native of my hometown, for agreeing to read the manuscript and for correcting inaccuracies about historical events.

My thanks to the entire publishing staff of Yad Vashem for seeing the book through to print.

Prologue

"Grandma, tell me your stories again, about when you were really little and about when you were my age. I want you to start from the beginning and not leave anything out. Last time you left out all kinds of things and I had to remind you... Grandma, maybe you could write it all down, and then for sure you won't forget anything!"

That was the request of my eleven-and-a-half-year-old granddaughter. Who could say no to her and disappoint those big, expectant blue eyes?

During my many years as an elementary school teacher and as an instructor in teachers' colleges, I was invited each Holocaust Remembrance Day to tell my story to students of various ages. It was always an emotional encounter; the empathy was overwhelming, and people came up to me afterward and asked me to put my story in writing. They urged me to seize the day, saying that as long as the last survivors are still alive and capable of telling and documenting their stories, they have a duty to do so. These arguments finally convinced me.

In fact, for a long time, well before I became a

grandmother, I felt a constant need to set down the story of what had happened to my family and me, everything that was stored and suppressed within me and was crying to be let out. I felt the need to preserve our story, to write things down before it was too late, before old age took over and memory faded, and my granddaughter's wish could no longer be fulfilled. But, like everyone else, I was caught up in the day-to-day routine. Time rushed by, and the unrealized promise continued to prick at my conscience. Still, I knew the time would come when all the events, fears and grief of the past would well up and burst through the silence; when everything would surface from the depths of my memory and appear to me vividly.

All things have their appointed time. Perhaps it was necessary for me to reach an advanced age, retire, and release myself from the daily routine for things to ripen within me and for the time of summing up to arrive.

In two years, I will turn 70. My memory already plays tricks on me sometimes; it tends to preserve mainly the most striking events of the past. Still, things that happened more than half a century ago remain engraved deep within my consciousness. All it takes is certain sights, voices, scents — tree branches swaying in the wind or the rustle of falling leaves in fall, the smell of hay in the field, a low window reaching almost to the sidewalk, the sound of church bells — and the old scenes are immediately evoked.

Yet, how, and where, does one begin?

"Grandma, why don't you start with the time when you were a little girl. And when I grow up and am a mother, too, it

will all be written down and I can tell my children the story…"

My granddaughter's persistence gives me strength. I plunge into the world of memories and begin to salvage my story.

School

(Autumn 1936)

Michalovce is a small town in eastern Czechoslovakia. About a third of its 15,000 residents were Jews. A magnificent synagogue stood in the center of town, opposite the Town Hall. The sanctity of the Sabbath was felt even on the main streets, as the shops owned by Jews were closed from the advent of Shabbat on Friday afternoon until the holy day was ushered out the next evening. In fact, most of the residents on the main street were Jews. The town secretary and the majority of the doctors, engineers and other intellectuals were Jewish.

The Jewish community was almost entirely Orthodox or traditional; only a small minority were secular. Most of the Jews lived in the same neighborhood, in apartment buildings built around long courtyards. Each courtyard was home to ten or twelve families, all in very modest apartments. Usually the lavatory was not in the apartment, but at the edge of the courtyard. Each courtyard was inhabited by either Jews or Christians only. My family lived in one of the courtyards on the main street, across from the

Great Synagogue, with another ten families. We were three sisters: At six, I was the eldest; my sister Rachel, who was four, attended kindergarten; and Miriam, the baby, stayed home with a nanny.

In 1936, life proceeded smoothly. There were as yet no signs of the impending disaster. The Jews, who lived in densely crowded conditions that all but ruled out privacy, felt that Michalovce was their home, as had the many generations of Jews who had lived there before them. We didn't know it, but the sand of the hourglass was already running out, grain by grain, signaling the end of our tranquil life and the arrival of an ominous, frightening future. Rumors filtered in that the Jews in enlightened Germany were being treated harshly and that there was a mass flight from that country, but this seemed to have nothing to do with Jews in other places.

In 1936, I entered first grade in the general, municipal, non-Jewish school. It was a very special, emotional event. My parents did not accompany me on my first day of school, because that was not the custom where we lived. Maybe they trusted me, or maybe they just didn't give the matter much thought. A few of us girls from the neighborhood walked to school together, to give one another moral support.

I had a strange custom that I performed every morning, and that I have not really abandoned to this day: When I awake in the morning, the first thing I do is to look toward the window, as I did when I was a child in Michalovce. In those days, I saw a large tree that was framed by the window. It was a kind of ritual—to greet the tree every morning, as though it heralded the new day and blessed it. The tree that grew outside my bedroom window symbolized something enduring and stable, something deeply known and calming. I observed the changes the tree went through as the seasons unfolded. Sometimes I had the feeling that the tree was a living creature you could talk to.

I looked after myself from a very young age, maybe because I was the eldest. So, from the first week of school, I knew I had to get up early. I was always the first to wake up. My parents, who slept in the next room, knew I was a responsible girl and could get dressed by myself and say the *Modeh Ani* prayer of thanksgiving—as I did every morning, even before getting out of bed. Preparations for school were always done the day before. My new schoolbag lay on the chair next to the bed. It contained only one book, a reader, along with a pen-and-pencil case and two notebooks, one for reading lessons and the other for arithmetic.

In those days, reading was taught by the phonetic method, without paying attention to what the words meant. Each page in the book was devoted to a different letter of the alphabet, and every day we learned a new letter. After we knew the sound, name and shape of all the letters, we memorized them and recited them monotonously. It was only when we reached the end of the book that the letters came together into words that had meaning. I found this boring, but I really loved arithmetic. I could count and do addition. I liked to show off what I knew already from the time I was in kindergarten. In reading, I was less brave and I had a hard time with the spoken language—because my mother's native tongue wasn't Slovakian, which was the language used in the school I attended.

My mother had come to Slovakia from Hungary in order to marry; it was an arranged match, as was the custom then. She didn't know the local language. Apart from a few sentences she needed for shopping and for the sewing salon she set up and managed, she never did master Slovakian, even though my father spoke it. Fortunately, mother could get along quite well in our region with her Hungarian and German, as the local Jews were fluent in both languages. We spoke Hungarian at home. I spoke Slovakian poorly, based on what I picked up in the kindergarten I attended for a short time, and from playing with neighboring children. My language deficiency showed mainly in school, and it bothered me anew every morning on the way there.

It was a dull, gray autumn day; a cold wind lashed my face and stung my ears. The wind shook the branches of the trees in a kind of rhythmic dance. Like the arms of dancers, the branches moved up and down, right and left, scattering the already yellowing leaves. Gusts of wind flung the leaves around in circles before they drifted to the ground. It was a wonderful sight, which still has a hypnotic effect on me when I recall it.

On the way to school, I encountered many children who were also hurrying to the low building with the tiled roof and rectangular windows overlooking the street. At the gate, I marched in with all my classmates. We entered the classroom, took off our coats and sat down in our places, waiting for the ringing of the bell that announced the start of the lesson. We sat in pairs in two rows, waiting. At last the door opened and the teacher stood in the doorway. The children rose and total silence descended upon the classroom.

"Good morning, children," the teacher said.

"Good morning, teacher," we replied in unison.

"Be seated," the teacher told us, and we all sat down and folded our arms.

"Before we learn the letter 'D,' everyone stand up, put the palms of your hands together and we will start our day with the Ave Maria prayer."

The children all began to recite the prayer. Only I, along with my best friend Yehudit and another few Jewish girls, stood there silently. We kept our heads bowed, our hands drooping listlessly by our sides, our eyes downcast. I was embarrassed, conscious that I was different, and restlessly shifted my weight from one foot to the other, all the while peeking at the teacher uncomfortably. When our eyes met, I felt uneasy, as though I saw reproach in her look. Without my intending to, my lips began to mumble the words of the Christian prayer, which I had picked up, even though I knew it was not my prayer. Jewish children were officially excused from reciting Christian prayers, and the Jewish community provided us with a teacher of Judaism in the afternoon. Still, we had to be present and stand up with everyone during the class prayers. It was difficult and unpleasant. I felt the curious eyes of the non-Jewish children on me; I was ashamed and felt that I didn't belong. The prayer seemed to go on for a long time and I kept wishing it would end so we could start the lesson. The estrangement from Christianity that I felt then in those morning prayers has never left me; it is instantly evoked whenever I hear Christian prayers being recited.

At last the prayer was over and we were told to take out the book, along with writing utensils and notebooks, and the lesson began. Suddenly, only a few minutes after we started repeating words after the teacher in chorus, someone knocked on the door. We fell silent immediately and everyone looked toward the door. At a signal from the teacher, we got up and stood quietly. The door opened and a third-grade teacher entered, along with a boy who looked too old for the third grade. The teacher held the boy by the ear and he stood shamefacedly by her side. His patched clothes were too small for him and his shoes were caked with dried mud. He had blond hair and his head was bent, his gaze fixed on the floor.

The teacher in the doorway said, "Good morning, children, you may be seated." After letting go of the boy's ear, she continued: "Do you see Jan? Jan is a pupil in my class, in third grade. Jan is very lazy and doesn't know arithmetic. I brought him to first grade so he can see that even children in first grade know how to solve an exercise that is so hard for him, so he will be ashamed. I asked him how much is six plus seven and he didn't know the answer. Is there anyone here who can tell stupid and lazy Jan the answer?"

Our teacher scanned the class, then pointed to me, and said, "Are you ready to tell this stupid boy how much six plus seven is?" I knew the right answer right away, but I didn't know how to say "thirteen" in Slovakian, so I replied, unsure of myself, "Ten, three." The children burst out laughing and I wanted to disappear into the ground, I felt so ashamed. But our homeroom teacher came to my aid. "Quiet, children!" she said. "Aliska's answer is correct, the answer is really thirteen. It's only a pity she still isn't fluent in our beautiful language. In any case, Jan learned something from her, and he should be ashamed that a little girl from first grade can do arithmetic better than he can." My heart was pounding and my face burned with mixed feelings of satisfaction and embarrassment. Then the "spectacle" ended. The third-grade teacher pushed Jan toward the door, we stood up again in her honor, and after they left the lesson continued normally.

At the end of the school day, we collected our things, put on our coats and hats, and, after saying goodbye in unison, we left the classroom in pairs. Outside, everyone happily went his own way. I always left together with Yehudit, my friend and neighbor. But that day, Jan suddenly jumped out at us from between two houses, brandishing a stick in his hand. He ran over to us. We were terribly frightened and started walking back toward the school. He shook the stick at us and shouted, "Stinking Jew-girl, I'll show you what it is to shame me in front of the whole first grade! You're really smart in school, but let's see you now, without the teacher to protect you!" He swung the stick hard and hit me on the shoulder. A sharp pain sliced through my thin body and I fell backward. If not for my thick coat, which softened the blow, I would have been badly hurt. We started crying and running, but Jan was faster, and again the stick landed on me — this time on my head. Fortunately, an adult passed by and Jan ran away.

I came home bruised and crying, and told my parents what had happened. My head hurt a lot, but the worst thing was the burning insult of being called a "stinking Jew-girl." That was the first time anyone had ever said anything like that to me. My parents and the whole community were quite upset over the incident, but thought it was an isolated event. Most people preferred to forget about it. My parents complained about the boy to the headmaster and, with that the disgraceful episode ended and was forgotten by them, too.

For a long time after the incident, I felt frightened on my way to and from school. I kept looking around for fear that Jan would suddenly appear again and hit me. But the warning he got from the principal did the job and he left us alone. I continued to attend a municipal general school until 1939, and more and more insults were hurled at us, the Jewish children.

In the 1939-1940 school year, all the Jewish teachers were dismissed from the general schools. A young but distinguished educator, a native of our town who had taught in another community for years, saw the writing on the wall. He returned to our town and courageously and resourcefully initiated the establishment of a Jewish school. The more enlightened community leaders assisted him, and he began spreading the idea and trying to organize the project. It was not easy. The authorities, who were already under the influence of German antisemitism, blocked any possible help. Also, there was no suitable building, and basic equipment was lacking. There weren't enough trained teachers in the community, as some of the teachers had been conscripted into the army, and teachers had to be brought from distant locales, which was very problematic in those days.

However, the biggest obstacle was the arguments between the different currents in the Jewish community about what type of school it should be: Would there be mixed classes with both boys and girls? What would the division be between sacred and secular studies?

The opening of the school was delayed by the German invasion of Poland, which touched off the Second World War. However, thanks to the tenacity of the young educator (who became headmaster), most of the obstacles were overcome and following an intensive organizing effort, an independent Jewish school was founded in Michalovce.

The Jewish children transferred from the general schools to the new Jewish institution. We noticed the change of atmosphere right away; we felt a release from the fears and anxieties that had gripped us. Our joy was real, despite the miserable physical conditions. The new school strengthened our Jewish and Zionist consciousness. Before long, all Jewish children were expelled from the municipal schools, and it was only thanks to the headmaster, who had read the situation correctly, that there was a school they could attend. The majority of the Jews did not consider the separation an insult; in fact, they were pleased that their children were protected from attacks and bad influences. No one imagined that these were the first signs of a dark period that would end with persecution, destruction and annihilation.

How many signs must there be before a person understands what is coming? In the face of the furious storm that was rapidly approaching and already swirling across vast areas, the Jew stands, his eyes closed, his head buried in the sand despite bitter, generations-long experience, and exclaims, "With God's help, all will be well!"

The Man in the Wall

World War II broke out in September 1939. Half a year earlier, in the wake of the Munich Pact, the German army crossed into Czechoslovakia and seized Bohemia and Moravia. In Slovakia, which was separated from Czechoslovakia with the support of the Germans, the Jews suffered from the political developments. Anti-Jewish laws followed one another in rapid succession. Jews were dismissed from government jobs, commercial firms and banks, and the land of wealthy Jewish farmers and estate owners, whose families had lived for centuries in their villages, was taken from them and transferred to gentiles.

At the end of 1941, the situation became even worse. Many people lost their livelihood and no one knew what the following day would bring. Michalovce was one of the first places in eastern Slovakia where Jews from the age of six were forced to wear a yellow band on their left arm. Soon there was a brisk trade in preparing and selling the yellow patches. Overnight, we became marked and different.

In the Jewish communities, there was a great deal of whispering and arguing about the future. Some people still vividly remembered the terrors of World War I.

Strangers—mostly young people in their twenties—appeared on the streets and in the synagogues. Neighbors gathered in the courtyards to tell the latest news about these mysterious newcomers.

In our house, too, we heard rumors about Jewish refugees from Poland who had crossed the border at night and found shelter in towns where there was a Jewish population. Members of the community who heard their horrific accounts lost no time in telling others. Yet it was clear that, despite the understanding and the emotional identification with the distress of the refugees, there was a good deal of mistrust concerning their "stories." And really, how could anyone believe such things? The "Poles" told about how the Jews were concentrated into ghettos and about cruel and brutal treatment, including mass murder (the term "ghetto," in its full meaning, was unknown in Slovakia, although in Michalovce, too, many Jews were forced to leave their apartments on the main streets and move to even more modest dwellings on side streets). The refugees told of mass flight, particularly by young people, into Romania and Russia.

The community was deeply grieved at the news brought by the refugees and sympathized with them. However, the feeling was that this was something that could only happen "there." Poland was known for its powerful, centuries-old antisemitism and as a country that was eager to collaborate with the Nazi occupiers and their racist doctrine. Whereas here, in Slovakia, "It could never happen!" True, there was latent antisemitism, but the Jews' contribution to the economy of the town and the country ensured the community's well-being. The social involvement, joint schools, close neighborly relations and good relations with the Christians over so many years reflected the harmony and mutual dependence that existed between residents from all walks of life.

The refugees kept arriving in a constant trickle, and their accounts of the ordeals they had endured grew ever more appalling. We began to worry that we were trapped. Still, we continued to live normally, perhaps preferring to repress thoughts of the terrible future we feared. It was as though the Polish disaster was a problem that did not concern us. The Jews of Europe sealed themselves in a protective armor that kept the world out and they refused to believe what they were hearing. So nothing was done to prepare for what finally happened. Even before the events in Poland, Jews were expelled from Germany, Austria, and the Czech Republic, yet the Jews in our region were complacent, believing that they would be spared, that the storm would pass and that "everything would be fine."

The refugees gradually became integrated into the community. Each family undertook to provide for, and look after, one of the new arrivals. This was the situation until 1941. And then....

I remember coming home one day after school and suddenly feeling that it was not the same house any more: The expensive carpets were gone, and the wood floor, now bare, looked so strange, as though the old familiar colors had been removed from the room, leaving everything cold and alien. "What happened?" I asked, and was told that a municipal law had been passed obligating the Jews to hand over their carpets, paintings, and jewelry to help the war effort. Since Jews were not called up for military service—as they were considered unreliable—they had to contribute their share materially at least. The Jews were warned that if they tried to hide gold and silver objects (apart from wedding rings, which they were allowed to keep) they would face severe punishment. Even so, almost everyone took the risk and hid some valuables for the troubled times ahead.

Even Father, an avowed optimist who was always brimming with faith and hope, looked worried and careworn. And not because of the loss of the carpets, the paintings, or the jewelry—no, it was because of the radio, which also had to be turned over, to ensure that the Jews did not make use of secret political information and become a fifth column. During this whole period, Father had listened to the radio constantly, trying to glean every possible bit of information from the BBC broadcasts from London. Day and night, he listened compulsively for hours on end, hoping to hear encouraging news about the Allied forces and praying for salvation to arrive.

Nothing could be done: The order was to hand over the radio to the brutal enemy. But then a solution was found. Our gentile neighbor, a childhood friend of Father's, suggested that they switch radios. He would give father his radio, which was small and emitted mostly static, and father would give it to the authorities; in return, the neighbor would get our large, excellent radio and Father would be able to listen to the news occasionally when he visited. And that is what they did: the small radio was handed over to the authorities and Father listened to the news in the home of the gentile neighbor.

All these events were only the first signs of the harsh developments to come. It is important to understand that from the start, we were at the mercy of an unceasing flood of rumors. Some were false, but most turned out to be true, unfortunately. Every rumor, no matter how absurd, quickly made the rounds among the frightened Jews of the town, who feared what the future held in store. On Friday, March 1942, a rumor spread that all girls and unmarried women aged 16 and older were going to be taken away. No one knew the exact details.

The next day it was learned from a hasty telephone call that the girls in the neighboring town had been kidnapped, herded into railroad cars and sent to an unknown destination. It all sounded totally unreasonable, the product of a sick imagination. Were girls really being abducted in broad daylight in the middle of civilized Europe? Not even in the pogroms of the Cossacks had there been such a thing! A great abyss seemed to open up and people began to be afraid that this time something truly terrible was about to happen. Pure and virtuous girls who were strictly protected and never went anywhere unaccompanied would suddenly be wrenched from their families. The greatest anxiety was for the young girls. A great and bitter cry went up from the community, as though the sky had fallen on us. A day of fasting and prayer was declared. The atmosphere turned foul. What to do? Where to flee? Would the girls really be sent to work in central Slovakia? Or was it all a scheme to cover up something far worse?

At the beginning of March, there had been rumors about the labor camp at Ilawa, to which men with a political past, or who were suspected of sympathizing with left-wing parties, had been exiled. From there they were transported to the death camps. According to the rumors, the intention was to round up all the Jewish men in Slovakia and send them to Ilawa. Every family feverishly tried to save its young men at any cost. Many men, even some who were married, fled across the border into Hungary. But what about the girls? What would become of them? No one had ever imagined that these helpless creatures would be among the first to be taken. And what did they want from the girls, anyway? What could girls contribute to the war effort? The looming horror of the onrushing calamity paralyzed everyone and threatened to tear apart families and the whole community.

On Sunday, the main street was deserted. A heavy silence prevailed. The women and girls stayed inside, in the protective fold of their families. The next morning, Michalovce resembled a town under siege. The streets were filled with soldiers and armed police. Had all these troops arrived in order to fight enemy battalions or well-organized rebels? After all, these were only young Jewish women and girls!

To ensure that the mission would be carried out fully and faithfully, the authorities sent in the Hlinka Guard, a military unit that was loyal to the ruling party, like the SS in Germany. The troops wore black uniforms and high, shiny boots, and the sight of them struck fear and terror in everyone's heart.

To prove their loyalty to the Third Reich, these Slovak *gardists*, as we called them, tried to outdo the Germans in cruelty. Their assault on the girls and young women, whom they trapped in their homes, was shockingly brutal. The police and soldiers tore the girls from their mothers' arms, dragged them away without any mercy or compassion, crammed them into trucks and took them to the railway station. Mothers threw themselves in front of the trucks, but the barbarians struck them with their rifle butts and chased them off. Grief-stricken parents ran about in the streets helpless, sounding heart-rending cries and begging for mercy, but to no avail. The non-Jews, who looked on as the events unfolded, did not so much as lift a finger to save the girls. For three days and three nights the hunt went on, and the few who managed to elude the troops were taken later, with their families.

We would often hear the sound of a drum in the streets — that was the usual way of making announcements about administrative orders of all kinds that the residents had to obey. One such announcement ordered all Jewish men from the age of 16 to report to the town square; from there they would be sent to work, to help the army. Each person could take up to 30 kilograms of food and clothing in a knapsack. By fulfilling this duty, the Jews would make their contribution to the war effort.

Again, the Jews were thunderstruck. Speculation and arguments were rife in the synagogues. The men often came home late, as though the evening prayer went on into the night. Quietly, people wondered about the order and asked one another whether to obey and report to the town square, or to hide and flee. The ground no longer felt steady under people's feet. Most of the Jews had believed they were safe and protected in the towns where they and their ancestors were born. Now, as with the expulsion of the girls, the Jewish community faced a huge question: What were the authorities' true intentions? Where would they be sent? Would they really serve in the army? What would happen to the families who were left without males? Who would provide for and protect them?

A few young men fled into the forests and joined the partisans who were beginning to organize there; they were trained in resistance and sabotage methods, though they did not yet have any outside help. A few members of my father's family—my bachelor uncle and some cousins—decided to join the fighters. They came in the dead of night to say goodbye and receive the blessing for a safe journey. So the unattached men in my family left and fled into the unknown. My uncle Menachem, though, hesitated, and at the last moment decided to stay, in the hope that he would be able to find a hiding place and elude the authorities.

Father was extremely frustrated. It went without saying that he would not flee and abandon his family, even though he might be taken for the army operations—and then be compelled to leave a wife and three little girls with no protection. What should he do? Father was determined not to be sent away. He and Mother considered a few options, and finally decided on the one that seemed the most "possible" at that critical moment, a plan that was conceived, this time, by Mother.

Before going ahead with the plan, Mother and Father

told me about it one evening, after my two sisters were already sleeping. As the first-born, I was let in on the great secret, even if I was not yet twelve years old, because I had a part to play in the plan.

In the bedroom, which was the most spacious area in our small, two-room flat, a door on one of the walls led to a small walk-in closet, about four square meters in size. It had shelves on which bedding and winter clothing were stored, and it was sealed and windowless. The idea was that Father would hide there during the day and we would move the clothes closet in front of the door to hide it. In the evening we would move the closet back to its regular place and Father would come out to eat with us and maybe even sleep in his own bed.

Naturally we did not tell anyone about the plan — not even my little sisters, who might blurt it out unintentionally. Only I, the eldest, knew about it, because Mother needed my help every night to move the clothes closet from its temporary place so that Father could come out, and then move back the closet late at night, when the little ones were fast asleep.

And so it went. Toward evening, Father would come out, have a bite to eat and lie down for a rest — in the walk-in closet he could only sit, as there wasn't enough room to stretch out. All the while, Mother and I were on guard behind a closed door. If someone approached the house, we had to wake up Father immediately so he could return to his hiding place. After only two or three hours of desperate sleep, Father would return to the walk-in closet and the chair, while Mother and I closed the door, leaving it open just enough to let air enter. Then we moved the clothes closet back in place, to hide the door.

Three days passed. Most of the Jewish men prepared themselves to report as ordered, organizing the items they would need and the few clothes they could stuff into a knapsack. There was tension in the air. The children did not go to school. The adults walked about with worried looks, their eyes giving away the confusion and anxiety in their hearts.

At the appointed time, the men left their homes and started to walk to the town square. My sisters and I looked out the window and saw whole families walking down the main street toward the square. Among them we spotted many neighbors and people we knew. It was a pleasant spring day, and if not for the men's anxious faces and the crying of the mothers and wives who accompanied their sons and husbands, you might have thought that all these people were on the way to an outing or community celebration.

I watched with amazement as the people continued to stream past the window. I never knew there were so many Jewish men in our town. All this time, Father was shut in behind the closet. I felt a little embarrassed that we were not part of the crowd, as though I were missing some special experience that brought everyone together. I was almost angry that my father was the exception and not part of the crowd, and was instead hiding like a mouse in a hole.

After a while, the flow of people thinned to just a trickle. Then my curiosity got the better of me: I wanted to see what would happen next, and even though I was forbidden to leave the courtyard, I stole away and joined the walkers. The square where the men were to gather was close to our house. I ran all the way, promising myself that I would only have a quick look to see what was going on and then go back right away.

When I got there, I stood on the square stones, astonished at the large crowd that was packed into the open space. I looked around and I heard people crying and trying to comfort one another. I couldn't move. I felt like I was rooted to the spot. I don't know how long I stood there, just staring at the people, my mind a blank, until the sound of a drum suddenly snapped me out of my daze. As the rhythmic drumbeat continued, I grew tense and listened attentively.

An oppressive silence descended on the square. The drumming continued and then someone began to bark out orders. The men were told to say farewell to their families. Bodies were pressed close in embraces and everyone burst into heart-rending tears. Standing by myself in the packed square, I felt loneliness, fear and terror. I still shiver whenever I recall that scene. It comes back to me at night, in my dreams, and I wake up suddenly in a cold sweat.

More pounding on the drum, and then the order: "All the men, form pairs! Forward march! To the train station!" The crowd began to move, escorted by the local police. The women and children were not allowed to pass and were ordered to go back home. A few policemen even tried to reassure them: "What can we do?" they said. "There is a war on and the Jews have to take part, too. They will help the soldiers and at the end of the war they will return home safely." Thus the men of our town were sent to do forced labor together with the rest of the Jews of Slovakia.

After this first group, other groups were also sent to "work." These were mainly people who had tried to hide, but despaired because they had no food or water in their hiding places. This fraud of the work camps went on for almost a year—until the first letter arrived from the ghettos of Poland with a description of the harsh conditions in the concentration camps, which had nothing to do with helping the army. When the deportees from Slovakia arrived in the concentration camps, they found Jews from Poland who had been imprisoned earlier. In the camps they were forced to work in extreme conditions of hunger and cold, and anyone who did not have the strength and spirit to continue, simply collapsed and died, or was "liquidated." We knew nothing yet about sophisticated, planned mass extermination.

The children in the town continued to attend the Jewish school, as though everything was the same. In fact, we usually felt safer among the children and teachers at school than we did at home. The school routine made us concentrate on our studies and not think about the problems of the adults. Being among the children was familiar and comforting; it brought a welcome forgetfulness.

Our homeroom teacher was the headmaster himself, the very person who had initiated the Jewish school. He was very pedantic and strict, believed in conservative methods of education and imposed iron discipline. We all held him in awe, and sensed his distance and restraint. Yet one day we saw his spirit broken by pain and grief, and he suddenly seemed softer and more vulnerable.

That morning when he entered the classroom, the headmaster was dejected and self-absorbed, very unlike his usual self. We rose in his honor as always, but this time we looked at him curiously. In a near whisper, he said, "Be seated." Even his voice sounded different.

One brave boy had the nerve to ask, "What is it, Sir?"

And then something happened that made us freeze in our seats. This tough, formal man suddenly burst into bitter tears and said, between sobs, "My sister Esther" — she was a kindergarten teacher in our town — "was taken away and I am afraid I will never see her again."

We were stunned by his extraordinary behavior and the intensity of his tears, totally surprised by the tender, human side of the man that was revealed, and we were also terribly distressed by the news about his sister. We children (mainly the girls) also burst into tears. We laid our heads on the desks and cried for ourselves as well, as though sensing the calamity that was about to descend on us, too. After a while, the headmaster pulled himself together, asked us to calm down, and started the lesson as though nothing had happened. Not long before, he had married another teacher, Miriam, so she would not be sent on a transport — there had been many marriages for this reason. His sister apparently had not managed to marry.

Most of the girls and men in the town had already been transported, but the wealthy Jews and the community leaders could still buy their freedom for a large ransom, which was their contribution instead of "work." We did not have enough money for this, so my father continued to spend his days in the tiny space behind the clothes closet.

Each new day brought new fears for the future, and we were constantly afraid that he would be discovered.

The town authorities were not satisfied with the number of Jews who had reported for the transports and decided to search the houses of those who were on the list but had not turned up. They knocked on every door to which a *mezuza* was affixed (People joked that we were back in the days of bondage in Egypt, when the first-born were struck dead — though the difference was that then the Angel of Death had passed over the houses of the Israelites). We knew it was only a matter of time before the dreaded knock would be heard on our door, too.

And then, one evening, it happened. The door was opened violently. Two men in uniform burst into the house and asked Mother, "Where is your husband, Moritz?"

Mother understood the question but couldn't answer because she was not fluent in Slovakian. Spontaneously, without any prior plan, I thrust myself between Mother and the policemen, and said, "My mother doesn't speak Slovakian well. I will translate and answer you." When they repeated the question, I said, "Father escaped into the woods with some other people."

I tried hard to look self-confident and not to blink, but my heart was pounding. I was sure the *gardists* could see right through me and knew I was lying.

I felt like I was going to pass out, and then one of them grabbed me viciously by the arm, scowled at me and said: "I don't believe you. It will be too bad for you if you lied to us and we find your father in the house!"

After he let go of me, I swallowed all the saliva that had

built up in my mouth and I looked at Mother—she was white as a sheet and her teeth were rattling from fear. In her eyes, though, I saw approval for my brave behavior. The *gardists* looked in every corner of the house and in the courtyard, too. They searched beneath the closets, but fortunately they did not find the opening to the hidden room.

Mother sat down, almost faint with fear, and my sisters woke up and started to cry. The *gardists* turned to them, too—"Where is your father?"—but as they did not know the secret they could not give us away. The search went on and on. It seemed endless, and just when they were about to leave, one of them again threatened me angrily: "If your father comes back, you have to tell him that he must report immediately, and then he will not be punished; if we find out that you didn't do as you were told, you will all pay dearly!"

When they finally left the house, we collapsed on the floor, totally exhausted, and cried bitterly—partly in relief that things had ended well and partly in fear of the future. What would happen tomorrow, and the next day? Father had heard everything from his hiding place behind the wall, and that night he told us he had almost been tempted to come out in order to protect us, because he was afraid the *gardists* would hurt us when they couldn't find him.

Father hid in the little room for a long time and came out between one transport and the next. It was only by chance that he wasn't caught and sent to a concentration camp in Poland. After the young women and most of the men in the town were taken to "work"—deceitfully, as we learned later—came the turn of the families. Who did they intend to take for work this time? The children? The pregnant women, or women with families? Maybe the old people, too?

A few weeks after the deportation of the young people, the Jews from the villages were forced into the towns and cities, where the *gardists* could round them up more easily. Now everything was ready for the deportation of the families. The women were told that now they would be able to join their husbands and sons and daughters, and many people looked forward to the day of the transport, happy about the upcoming "family reunification." This was understandable: Many women who had remained alone with their children were having serious economic difficulties and suffering mentally as well. They were in despair at being separated from their husbands and preferred any solution to the situation as it was. As before, quite a few people paid the right officials and were given documents exempting them from deportation.

The story repeated itself. We did not have enough money to ransom ourselves from the transports. In the meantime, Father had stopped hiding in the little room, because the transports of men had stopped, but mainly because he wanted to be with us in case we were all sent away. Once again we were weighed down by the feeling of having nowhere to turn. Mother and Father talked and argued for hours every night, trying to find a solution so we would not be deported. But what could we do? One thing was certain: we could not all fit in the small storeroom, and even if we could, who would look after us there? We urgently had to find some other solution—and so began the next chapter in the story of our rescue.

The Bell

At the beginning of 1942, even before the deportation of families began, the Jews started to look for ways of escape and rescue. People who made great efforts and understood how the system worked sometimes were able to find a solution, even if it was only temporary. For example, it was possible to buy a permit to remain, but this was very expensive and only the wealthy could afford it. Others tried to get across the border, but this sometimes ended in tragedy — those who were caught were almost routinely shot on the spot. Many families paid non-Jews large sums of money for help and shelter, and this saved some of them from the transports, if only for short periods.

For the same reason, a plan was organized to issue fictitious "baptismal certificates," though they were only valid for a limited period. Mother obtained such a certificate, though without Father's knowledge, as he was absolutely against documents that involved conversion, even "pretend" papers. There were endless arguments on the subject in our house and in all the Jewish courtyards: "Better to die a martyr's death than to be saved by renouncing the faith, even if this is not genuine." But Mother, who protected her children as a lioness protects her cubs, was determined to save us, even if her conscience bothered her for ignoring Father's demands. However, this possibility of rescue was also soon closed, and it was no longer necessary to close one's eyes or be lenient toward the "new Christians." To this day, I ask myself whether Father guessed the reason we were not placed on one of the first transports, or whether he deliberately chose not to think about it.

As the mass transports were being organized, a new law came into effect that allowed some Jews to receive an exemption. Among the fortunate people who benefited under this law were specialists in medicinal herbs, experts in the manufacture of medical instruments and others. As before, wealthy individuals could still buy their freedom with money. The "privileged" Jews were ordered to wear on their outer garment a small, yellow Star of David made of Bakelite, like a kind of brooch. The letters "HZ," which stood for "Essential Jew," were printed on the tag and differentiated them from all the other Jews, who wore a large yellow cloth patch.

This time, thanks to the tag, our family too was able to remain in the town—for a short time, the authorities told us—instead of being sent to the camps.

The experts with the tags had to teach a non-Jew the main points of their profession, and quickly. The gentiles who were chosen as "students" were not necessarily eager to learn; they were being rewarded for their political loyalty to the fascist regime. Most of them were not residents of the town, but came from remote, poor rural areas. They were given apartments (the homes of Jews who had already been expelled) and also declared the legal heirs of the business and of their employer. The official name given to these people was *arizator*.

Father was among the fortunate few whose occupation spared them from being sent to the concentration camps. He had a workshop for making orthopedic aids to relieve various physical ailments; the devices were manufactured according to the specifications of the orthopedists who treated the patients. Since Father was the only person in the district who knew how to make them, he was a regular visitor to the hospitals and worked with them. He too was assigned a gentile "apprentice", who moved with his family from the north of the country to the town and who were housed in one of the apartments that now stood empty in our courtyard—the home of a Jewish family that had been sent to the East. The gentile and his family "inherited" the house and all its goods. Father became the man's employer and instructor, even though the newcomer understood nothing about the work, showed no special interest in the profession and made no serious effort to learn it, as his main occupation was politics. He was very pleased at having received an apartment for free and he was also promised a handsome salary for very little effort. Father and his *arizator* reached an agreement on the apprentice-heir's monthly salary, even though it was obvious that he was not going to learn the profession. His idleness pleased Father, because as long as the man did not become an expert in the work, we would not be deported. So time passed and the authorities kept extending Father's permit to remain in the town.

At the beginning of 1942, rumors spread that many Jews were smuggling their children into Hungary, where the Jews still lived in relative freedom and security. The smugglers were non-Jewish peasants who lived in villages near the border between Slovakia and Hungary.

My parents heard about a woman in one of these villages who had successfully smuggled people over the border for half a year. After my parents contacted her, she visited us secretly and they agreed on how much she would be paid. She was to get half the money on the day she took us and the rest when she showed Mother and Father a letter from our relatives in Hungary confirming that we had arrived safely. I was to go with my younger sister, Rachel; Miriam, the youngest, would stay with Mother and Father. But the little one started to cry, upset at having to stay. She begged to be allowed to go with us, as though we were going on some sort of pleasure outing. After a great deal of agonizing, Mother and Father relented and agreed to send Miriam with us. Mother was instructed to prepare a small knapsack of clothes, which would not be too heavy for young girls like us to carry on our back for a few hours during which we would cross the border on foot.

Mother prepared for the journey. She ordered us lovely festive dresses from a seamstress, bought us each a new pair of shoes, in addition to the ones we would wear, and also warm sweaters. Everything was packed and ready for the big day. On that day the village woman arrived at our house and I saw her for the first time. She was large and robust and wore native dress—colorful pleated skirts worn in layers one on top of the other, with each skirt broader than the one below, creating a kind of tent effect. Her head was covered with a multicolored embroidered kerchief, and she carried a wicker basket. Her shoes were crude and very large, with the top parts made of leather and wooden soles.

There was no time to lose, the woman said, and quickly explained the plan. She would carry our food and clothing in her basket, to ease the journey for us. At the train station she would buy the tickets and then give them to us. We would get on the train separately but sit in the same car — though not next to her. We were not to speak to her, so as not to arouse suspicion, until we reached her village. Of course, we removed the yellow patch, which was against the law.

We said our goodbyes quickly, so there would be no hesitation or regrets. We all fought to keep back our tears, but the pain of parting seemed to choke us as we embraced and received the blessing for a safe journey. Suddenly Miriam pulled her hand out of mine and broke into bitter tears, declaring between sobs that she did not want to go with us and wanted to stay with Mother and Father. No one tried to make her change her mind and my parents were obviously relieved that the decision to stay had been hers.

The farewell from Mother and Father was a difficult ordeal. A relative who was staying with us — her husband had been taken on one of the transports — took Mother to an inner room. Mother was hysterical, on the verge of fainting. She screamed and accused Father of sending his daughters to a sure death. Leaving home like this was a severe trauma for me. I remember it as though through a haze, and this memory is mixed with other farewells I went through during the war years. The memories of the grief and anxiety that accompanied these events are all buried in the depths of my consciousness.

We came to the train station. I used to love going on the train with my parents on vacation, to visit relatives or to travel to Grandmother in Hungary. But this time the train felt different, threatening. Hostile faces looked out of every window. Everyone seemed to know who we were. And really, it wasn't hard to guess our identity. Most of the local folk were fair-skinned with blond hair and blue eyes; we were darker and had brown-black eyes and dark hair.

We followed the woman into one of the cars. My sister held my hand, which was damp with tension. "Let's go home, I'm scared," she whispered to me in a panic. I told her there was no way back now and that I would take care of her, just as I had promised. In the car were peasants wearing colorful native dress and carrying straw baskets containing food and various items they had bought in our town. During the trip they took out some of the food and munched on it. We had food, too, but both of us had lost our appetite.

The sight of the ticket inspector made us anxious and alert. Would he notice that we were different? I glanced at him from the corner of my eye trying to guess his intentions. He was an older man, my parents' age, and wore the uniform and boots of the railway company; on his shoulder was a bag that was fastened by means of leather straps tied around his waist, and he held a ticket puncher. After punching the tickets of the other passengers, including the ticket of the woman who was escorting us, he turned to us, "Girls, are you alone?"

I replied a bit hesitantly, "Yes, we are going to visit our aunt in such and such a village." He looked around and cast his gaze on the woman who was taking us—she looked restless. Then he gave us another searching look and silently punched our tickets, shaking his head as though in disbelief before continuing to the next car. I am sure he guessed we were Jewish. Maybe he had children our age and so took pity on us. Whatever the reason, that encounter ended without incident.

After a slow journey and stops in many remote villages, we finally reached our destination. The woman signaled to us to follow her. We were the only three passengers who got off at this stop, which was almost the last one before the border. We started walking toward the village, which was a long way from the station. From afar the houses looked small and wretched, and only the church steeple, which towered above the village at one end, stood out because of its height and elegance. The way led through newly sown wheat fields, and the sprouting plants covered a large area. The trees were still bare, though the first buds could already be seen on the branches.

The sky was gray and dark, a perfect match for our mood. The woman hardly said a word and did not ask any questions, but she also made no effort to boost our gloomy spirits. She was certainly hard-bitten and hard-hearted. Evening began to fall, the sun had already set, and I expected that we would reach our destination very soon. Suddenly the woman stopped and said, "I see that people are still wandering about in the village. It's dangerous to take you into my house when it is still light outside and people might see us. Do you see that church over there? It is not far from here. We will go there and you will wait for me until after dark. Then I will come to take you to my house."

"And when will we cross the border?" I wanted to know. She said that if possible we would cross the border that very night.

As we approached the church, I felt a heavy sense of foreboding. This was not part of the agreement that my parents had reached with the woman in our presence. I was very upset that she was going to leave us, even abandon us—two frightened girls, in a strange place and in the dark. The tall, shadowy, cold building suddenly looked very unfriendly, even threatening. A large part of my uneasiness came from my deeply rooted resistance to anything Christian, which had been implanted within me from earliest childhood.

The front door turned out to be locked. We walked around the building until we came to a narrow side door, which was open. We stepped into a dark corridor from which a steep staircase led up to the steeple, at the top of which was a bell. The woman told us to follow her and started climbing the winding, narrow stairs. We clung tightly to the banister to keep from falling. The little light that penetrated through the opening in the steeple barely illuminated the twisting stairs. We climbed and climbed until we reached the top. Beneath the roof hung a huge metal bell that filled most of a small, square space, and beneath it was a wooden bench.

"Sit here and wait until I come to take you," the woman said without emotion.

My sister Rachel held on to me tightly. She was shaking and her eyes were wide with fright. I was also trembling all over at the thought that we would be left alone here, and in a place that was loathsome to every Jew, a source of hostility and hatred.

Crying, I begged the woman, "Please don't leave us here by ourselves! Don't go, stay with us until it gets dark."

But she explained coldly that she had to go home and make all the arrangements for the journey and see to it that nothing had gone wrong. She took the parcels with her, apart from the food, and told us to sit quietly and eat. She would be back soon, there was nothing to be afraid of. Then she turned and left without giving us another glance.

Silence fell, a silence so heavy it hurt our ears, and there was a stale smell in the air. We sat pressed against each other like two scared rabbits, awful thoughts racing through our minds. Every once in a while I looked up in terror at the huge, heavy bell that hung above us. Its vastness almost completely filled the little room in which we sat clinging to each other, almost petrified with fear. As we sat on the bench trying to comfort each other, we heard the door below open and then—quick footsteps. Thank heavens: the woman had returned. But a moment later we saw with horror that the bell hanging over our heads had begun to move back and forth—someone was pulling on the rope that was attached to it. The clapper pounded on the inner surface, making a sharp, metallic ring. The rope danced before our eyes and we watched as though hypnotized. The bell rocked from side to side and the clapper struck the sides with a booming, frightening sound.

We covered our ears with our hands to block out the deafening noise. After a time, the bell gradually stopped rocking back and forth until it finally stopped altogether. The sudden quiet made us alert and fearful of what would happen next — maybe whoever pulled the rope of the bell would come upstairs. Only when we heard the footsteps fading and then the door below closing did we understand that it was only someone who rang the bell to signal the end of the day.

I breathed a sigh of relief, but my sister started to cry and said in a broken voice, "Look at the bell, it is soon going to fall on our heads. I'm so scared, let's go down." As the big sister, I tried to calm her, but in my heart I agreed with her. I had exactly the same thoughts and was just as afraid as she was. Despite everything, I tried to get her to sit quietly and have something to eat. But she just kept crying, quietly and sadly, pressing up against me and cuddling in my arms. I was also choking with sobs, but in my role as the eldest and the responsible sister, I managed to hold back the tears. I was suddenly afraid that the woman would abandon us forever in the steeple. Wild and horrific images crossed my mind — we would be murdered and never found. After all, no one could prove anything or persecute the woman in this situation. How cruel of her to make us so terribly frightened. Didn't she have a God?

I don't know how long we sat there, embracing each other, freezing and trembling with fear in the hollow of the bell in that village church, but it seemed to last an eternity. Finally, though, we heard the door below open again and footsteps coming up. We were so tense we didn't even breathe—what if it was a stranger?! Rachel must have thought we had been plunged into a fairy tale, because she cried out, "Oh, listen, a witch is coming up the stairs, she is going to take us away! Oh, what is going to happen to us?" And she buried her head in my chest.

But it turned out to be the peasant woman, after all, her head wrapped in a kerchief. As soon as we recognized her, we stopped trembling. She gave us a look as though to say, You see, I came back, there was no reason to cry! We were very relieved, but immediately she gave us some bad news. People in the village were whispering about her, she said, and were suspicious about the smuggling operations. So she would not be able to take us to her home that night under any circumstances, and of course getting across the border was also out of the question for now. We would have to wait for a more suitable time.

"But what will happen now, what will become of us?" I asked hesitantly.

"There is one Jewish family in the village," the woman replied. "I will take you to them, and in the morning you will go back to the town, to your parents."

"How will we go back? Will you come with us?" I wanted to know, but seeing the angry look that crossed the woman's face I understood that she had no intention of accompanying us and that we would have to make our way back by ourselves, all alone.

By now it was totally dark, and the night that had fallen on the village seemed to have entered our very souls. Back on the street after going down the winding stairs, we could no longer see the houses, only faint lights shining out of distant windows. Silently we followed the woman, who again made no effort to allay our fears. She walked quickly and it was hard for us to keep up—holding hands, we almost had to run after her. Every once in a while she turned around and urged us to walk faster.

As we approached the houses, dogs started to bark furiously, which made us even more nervous. We walked for about fifteen minutes, but it seemed much longer. Finally we reached the first houses, and the woman knocked on the gate of one of them. A man holding a kerosene lamp came out and opened the gate. I could see that he was young and dark-skinned, wore clothes made of coarse cloth and had an especially large yarmulke on his head. He knew about us because the woman had been to see him earlier and they had reached an agreement. She had known he would agree, because even a simple village gentile woman like her knew that every Jew is obliged to help other Jews in distress.

The man invited us in. The whole house consisted of one large room with a low wooden ceiling. Beds stood next to two of the walls and in the center of the room was a simple wooden table with big chairs around it. There was a kitchen area with two large burners and a pipe between them that ran up to the roof and connected to the chimney.

The man looked at us with open curiosity and then smiled, as though telling us that we could trust him. He introduced himself and his young wife and emphasized that they were Jews—so it was clear we had nothing to fear. After hearing from the peasant woman that we were in trouble, they were ready to put us up in their home. I looked around some more and in a corner of the room I saw a cradle. It held an infant, who suddenly burst out crying. After a few minutes of mutual embarrassment, the woman of the house tried to comfort us, patting us on the head and offering us bread and butter with cheese, and milk. The peasant woman, seeing that the Jews had taken us under their wing and that she could be rid of us, got ready to leave. As she walked to the door, I asked her what had happened to the parcels with our new clothes and why she hadn't brought them with her. She replied that she hadn't wanted to make things difficult for us on the way here. She would return the parcels to our parents at the first opportunity, she said.

After the peasant woman left, we had a strange conversation with the young Jewish couple. They didn't really understand why we had come to their village, far from our home, without our parents. Why had we been sent away from home and what had made our parents want us to cross the border illegally into Hungary? I was very surprised at their questions — obviously, our parents were concerned for our safety and wanted to spare us from being deported.

We soon discovered that our young hosts were living in a kind of bubble and knew nothing about the calamity that had been visited upon the Jewish people across most of Europe and in Slovakia too. They had heard vague reports about various restrictions and prohibitions, about Jews being forced to wear a yellow patch, and about the mobilization of young men and women who were sent to assist the army and to work. But they had no clear knowledge about the decrees against the Jews of Slovakia. They had heard nothing about the deportations of the girls and the men, which had been going on for some time in the neighboring county, or about plans to exile entire families. When I told them about the rumors that whole families were going to be sent, with the promise that they would be reunited with the first groups of deportees, they refused to believe it. There was neither a telephone nor a radio in this remote village, and they had no information about the events. This solitary and peaceful family seemed to have been forgotten; the young man had not been sent on the first deportations.

The woman stared at us incredulously, as though we had made up this whole horrific story, and said, "I don't believe we will be taken from our home with our baby and sent to some unknown place. It simply can't be! Why should they do such a terrible thing? What have we done? The people in the village are our good neighbors and they won't let anything like that happen. We were born here, this is our home!"

How naive her declaration was. There was not a village in the whole of Slovakia where the gentiles raised an outcry or put up resistance to the brutal acts of deportation; only a very few helped the persecuted Jews. Later on, the *gardists* dealt mercilessly with every case such as the solitary family in this remote village, snatching them from their homes and transporting them to the camps with the rest of the Jews.

At this stage, though, the couple, whose name I have forgotten, tried to cheer us up. They urged us to eat and drink, gave us their bed to sleep in and covered us with quilts. Their tranquillity and warmth gave us critical psychological support and I have never forgotten them. We were so tired, worn out, and emotionally drained that we didn't even undress. We just took off our shoes and almost instantly fell asleep, hugging each other and feeling better, buoyed by the hope that the next day we would be going back home.

Early in the morning, while it was still dark, the young woman woke us up. She packed us food for the journey and embraced us, and her husband gave us money for train tickets. We had no money of our own. Before we left, this time alone, the man told us how to behave at the train station. He said he would walk with us almost to the station, and there we would part. We were to wait for the train, which would soon arrive, enter a car, find seats, and buy our tickets from the conductor when he made his rounds on the train. We would have to pay attention to make sure we heard the name of our town when it was called out, and get off as soon as the train stopped. The man said it would be better if he did not stay with us, as that would make it easier for us to hide the fact that we were Jews. We parted with mixed feelings. We were afraid of making the trip alone, but we were happy to be going home.

Again we found ourselves alone in the small, deserted station, which had only a narrow, flimsy platform. When the train arrived we entered a car that was almost empty and sat by a window. Again I was seized by fear. What if they found out we were Jewish? Would we get home safely without being arrested by the police? It was the first time in my life I had ever traveled alone, and here I was without even a permit, and with a little sister who was weepy and shaking with fear. But we had no problem buying the tickets, and the monotonous swaying motion of the train soothed us and even made us drowsy.

In fact, I was afraid we would fall asleep and miss our stop. Rachel leaned on me, crying softly until she fell asleep. I tried my best to stay awake, even pinching myself from time to time (as we were jokingly told to do at home when we felt drowsy, tired or sluggish).

At last I saw a large sign with the name of our town. The train slowed down, then stopped, and we got off quickly. A few hours must have gone by, because it was already almost noon. The sun shone brightly and we felt a pleasant warmth as we started walking. We had a long way to go, because the train station was on the outskirts of town. Then we started to run as fast as we could toward the town center, and we soon reached our house. We opened the gate and in another second we were at the entrance to the apartment. I can reconstruct this scene in full detail even today, 55 years later. It was Friday. The Jewish housewives were baking *challot* for Shabbat. Mother, too, had baked a *challah* every week for as long as I could remember. But when we entered the kitchen a strange scene greeted us. My aunt—the one whose husband was taken in one of the first transports—a big, hearty woman, stood there, legs spread apart, her large hands kneading the *challah* dough in a wooden pail. Next to her were two cradles, in each of which lay an infant. Her eldest son stood by her side, holding on to her skirt.

Mother sat next to the pail, staring vacantly into space. When she saw us, she let out a short, shrill scream, clasped her hands and said, "What is this, am I dreaming? Is it my imagination? Have I gone out of my mind? How did they get here and what are they doing here?" Even when we went over to her and held her tightly, she couldn't believe it. Then Father came in and we all embraced and cried from joy and sadness. Mother and Father said that this was apparently the way it had to be, that it was ordained by heaven. In short, "It's all for the best!"

Sobbing, we told them about our adventures. We said the woman had been cold and distant toward us and had even stolen our clothes and taken the money she had received as a downpayment. But Mother and Father consoled us, saying, "It doesn't matter, what's important is that you are here, safe and sound, and that nothing bad happened to you." Suddenly I was overwhelmed by a strange premonition; I understood that the house to which we had returned was no longer a safe haven.

Many years have passed since then, more than half a century, but whenever I am abroad and hear a bell tolling in a church or see a bell hanging in a church steeple high above my head, I am thrust back to that time with my little sister in the small space under the terrifying bell, where we were abandoned so traumatically for many hours.

Hiding in the Attic

In those days, when few people in our town had a radio or a telephone, the authorities made their orders known by means of a drummer, who would inform us that he was about to make an important announcement by beating on his drum. Everyone then had to gather at a designated place in order to hear the announcement. The crier would take out a scroll of paper, unroll it, and read out the new decrees. It was useless to claim that you had not carried out a certain order because you did not know about it; an order that was read out by the crier was binding on everyone, as though it had been handed to each person individually.

One spring day in 1942, the sound of the drum drew us to the town square to hear a new proclamation. With fear and trembling, we heard an old-new decree: migration to the East would begin in two weeks. All the Jews had to prepare themselves, including families with infants, and even the sick, the disabled and the elderly. Everyone was to take food and water for three days and essential clothing. A limit was set on the weight of suitcases, bags and knapsacks. To calm the crowd, the proclamation added that after the Jews left, the locks of their apartments would be sealed with wax in order to prevent strangers from entering, and their contents would be safeguarded until they returned at the end of the war. Anyone who entered a home without authorization would be punished severely. The move was temporary, we were told, in order to reunify families whose husbands and sons had been sent to assist the army. The women, too, would be able to join in the war effort by doing work of various kinds.

Most of the families left willingly: the women and children hoped to be reunited with their loved ones. The naivete and trust in the promises of the authorities were due in part to the desperate plight of most of the Jewish families, who no longer had anyone to provide for them. The desire to be with their loved ones overrode doubts about the authorities' credibility. Still, some Jews were suspicious and decided not to report as ordered, but to wait and see what developed.

The mass transport and deportation of whole families began on Tuesday, May 5, 1942. The previous day, buses had appeared on the main street, bringing units of the Hlinka Guard in their black uniforms and their high, shiny boots. These brutal troops had been sent from the west of the country—perhaps because the Slovak government was afraid that the local thugs would turn softhearted and take pity on Jewish acquaintances. The soldiers spread across the town, sealed off the exits, and at night began removing families from their homes. Together with the local police, they herded the Jews into schools, and when enough people had been rounded up, they took them to the train station. There they crammed them into freight cars and the trains departed immediately, their passengers bound for annihilation.

Panic seized the community. In our courtyard, too, fragmentary reports were whispered about the deportation, which had begun during the night. Father no longer dared leave the house, but he and Mother thought that a little girl would be able to make her way through the streets without arousing suspicion. So on Tuesday they sent my sister Rachel to my aunt and uncle, who lived a few blocks away, to see how they were and ask what they planned to do. Rachel soon returned home, frightened, after running all the way, to announce that she had found the apartment sealed with wax. The Jews had already been taken from the houses on that street, my uncle and his family among them.

This mass deportation, in which the Jewish inhabitants were taken from every house and every hiding place, went on for three days and three nights. Yet, even in that terrible time the people with money and good connections obtained special permits that let them survive.

The troops were vicious and had lost every trace of humanity. They spared neither the very old, nor the very young, and behaved like wild animals. The deportees were taken to the local high school and spent three days in the schoolyard before being packed on a freight train and transported to the Lublin area in eastern Poland. Not long afterward, the first postcards arrived from them, containing clear hints about killing and starvation.

We spent those horrific days of deportation in constant fear, hiding in the attic, to which we fled when we heard the pitiful cries in the streets. Then Father again received a temporary permit — it was always temporary — stating that he was an "essential Jew" for the state economy, which allowed us to come out of hiding. I have no clear memories of those days; they must have been so traumatic that they were wiped out of my consciousness altogether.

Despite the deportations, we children continued to attend the Jewish school, and it was only there that we were able to forget the tension and fear for a few hours, under the illusion that everything was normal. But every morning we carefully counted the number of pupils who arrived, because every day there were fewer of us. I walked to school every day with my good friend Yehudit who lived in the next courtyard. We had grown up together and I admired her beauty and self-confidence. She was at least half a head taller than me, a lovely, slim girl with two thick braids that fell all the way to her waist. As we crossed the main street, both of us marked with the yellow patch, I would cling to her in order to draw courage and a feeling of safety from her. But now, even she seemed to have lost something of her pride and to be less strong. Yehudit came from one of the wealthiest families in town; her father had good connections with the city elders and her family was always able to ransom itself from the transports.

As we walked to school, we would try to guess which of the children would be missing today and how many of us would be left by the end of the week. Because there were fewer and fewer pupils, four classes were combined into one. Where once there had been 140 pupils in fifth grade, we were now only about 15, so we joined the fourth and sixth grades. We studied at three levels of difficulty. Some of the teachers had been dismissed or deported, and the few who were left tried to make us forget the situation and to teach us what they could. One of the subjects they concentrated on was Zionism. We sang Hebrew songs, which we already knew from the Zionist youth movements, we listened to Bible stories and tales from the Jewish sages, and we also had religious lessons and learned how to use the siddur, the prayer book. We knew about the struggle that the small Yishuv—the Jewish community in Palestine—was waging against the British for its independence far away in our homeland.

Hardly a day went by without a boy or girl from our class disappearing. To avoid anxiety, we didn't ask questions or talk about the situation that existed outside the school. But every day I thought to myself that tomorrow I, too, might disappear. We knew that some of the missing children had been taken in the transports and that others had gone into hiding or had fled across the border.

Then came the day we had feared: we were told that Father's permit as an "essential Jew" had expired and that we could expect to be taken to the camps. Father, though, did not submit and looked for a way out. The hiding place in the attic, where we had gone when the deportations began, seemed to him a reasonable solution; after all, it had been a safe haven only a few months earlier. So we decided to hide in the attic, where we and the few neighbors who still remained hung laundry during the winter and on rainy days. An area that had not yet been used for hiding was chosen. The long space beneath the roof extended across all the attached apartments in a single row; there were a few such attics in the space under the roof.

The last of these, at the end of the row of apartments, was reached from a large storeroom, in which the tenants kept wood that was used as heating fuel in the cold winter months. This area was separated by a concrete or stone wall from the main attic above the row of apartments, and an isolated space existed there, without a passage, which was used mainly for storage. From here there was an opening to the roof, which was usually sealed by boards that were set into the beams of the ceiling. Anyone who didn't know this opening would not be able to guess that it was a way to get to the roof. When broken tiles or some other damage on the roof had to be repaired, a ladder would be placed under the opening and the wooden beams moved, to permit access to the roof. Afterward the ladder would be removed and the opening sealed again.

One night we climbed the ladder to the roof, where we hid with three other families. It was all done in silence and very cautiously, using only a flashlight, with someone keeping watch outside. Our family was the largest — mother and father and three girls. There was another family with a boy of about 14 or 15, a young couple who had just married, and one more family that joined us the next day. We planned to remain here for two or three days, until the manhunt ended.

We lay down on straw mattresses that had been brought to the place earlier and tried to sleep. We lay in a row, side by side. I heard the sighs and the heavy breathing of the others, and the noise made by mice that crisscrossed the floor. But we children fell asleep almost at once. The next day we were told to be quiet and we spoke in whispers. The men prayed, the women spoke quietly, and the children tried to hear what they were saying. Every once in a while we stood on tiptoe and looked down at our courtyard through cracks in the roof.

Suddenly we saw policemen enter the courtyard. They went from apartment to apartment, sealing the door of every empty apartment with wax—to show that the house was vacant and was now the property of the municipality. Besides those who were in hiding, there were some families from the courtyard who remained in their homes and would become part of the large group that was sent to the East. The family of the landlord, who paid a ransom and received permission to stay in their apartment, remained in the courtyard along with another privileged family.

We told the leaders of the community who were still free about our hiding place, and they organized "delivery boys" to bring us food after dark. The mission was assigned mainly to youngsters, some of whom were my classmates.

It was impossible to wash ourselves or to change clothes. We relieved ourselves in buckets, and everyone turned their head until the agreed signal was given that the person was finished. Of course, we children peeked, and laughed uproariously to see the grown-ups going to the toilet.

I remember the shock I got when I saw our pious neighbor, who wore a wig because of the religious injunction that women must cover their hair, sitting down to relieve herself in public. There was something repulsive about this, and deep inside I felt that we were losing the educational norms we had been raised on. At times there was a tremendous stench because we could only empty the buckets when the "delivery boys" brought us our food, and the buckets were returned unwashed and still smelling. After the first couple of days we began to become restive and despairing of the endless waiting.

The only place you could stand up was in the center of the space, at the point where the two sloping sections met. So we spent most of our time sitting or lying on the straw mattresses. We told stories, made up games, goofed around and played tricks. We rolled with laughter at the imitations and funny sounds made by the teenage boy who was with us. Our parents didn't care for this type of "entertainment" and scolded us for it.

Four days went by like this, one of which was the "Black Sabbath." We called it that because of what happened on that day. On Sunday evening, the day after, we received a huge delivery of excellent food with plenty of baked goods. The food had been prepared for the bar mitzvah celebration of a boy from our courtyard, whose family had a permit allowing them to go on living there. However, on the Shabbat when he was supposed to read from the Torah and afterward have the festive meal, the family's permit was canceled and they were ordered to report immediately for transport. So the Torah reading and the celebrations were canceled and we received the delicacies.

We children, of course, were delighted by this unexpected bounty and didn't really stop to think too much about how sad it was about the bar mitzvah. And we also ate most of the food. The adults cried and grieved over the tragedy, thanks to which we had a feast. Finally, when they could no longer bear their hunger, they ate a bit of food, but felt like traitors.

On the day before the eve of Tisha b'Av — the fast day on the ninth day of the Hebrew month of Av (which that year fell on July 23), commemorating the destruction of the First and Second Temples — my father declared that he had had enough of the attic, which was making everyone depressed. He suggested to Mother that we should sneak back into our apartment and sleep like human beings for one night, and then go back to the attic in the morning. Mother was against this, but after a fierce argument finally agreed to the plan. One after another we climbed down the ladder, which we dropped down from the attic and which, after we were all in the storeroom, was pulled back up, and the opening shut. The sun had gone down, though it wasn't yet completely dark — but we could wait no longer.

In total silence, almost on all fours, we made our way to our apartment. We left the wax seal untouched and entered instead through the window, which father managed to open. I remember clearly how happy and secure I felt as I stepped inside. The house was exactly as we had left it: things were scattered all over in a big mess, but it was a wonderful feeling to be back. Now we could sleep in our own beds. We also thought we would we able to bathe at last, but Mother and Father thought this was not the time for normal rituals like that. We were put to sleep by candlelight in our beds, and it felt like paradise.

The next morning we got up when the sun was already high in the sky and tried to plan what we would do next. We knew we could not stay for long in a closed and sealed apartment, without food. The only alternative was to go back to the attic. We had an opportunity to bathe and straighten up the apartment a little. While we were still thinking about what to do, someone suddenly passed by the window. We held our breath. My little sisters clung to Mother's legs and I stood next to the door, listening attentively. Father, who was extremely short-sighted and had very thick glasses, had the habit, especially when he was tense, of placing a finger on the frame of his glasses, above his nose, and pressing down a bit, as this helped him see better. Now he did just that and peeked out the window. He saw a shadow go by and immediately signaled us to be silent and bend down.

A moment later we heard tapping on the window and a voice said, "Open the door, it's me, Menachem."

Father pulled back the curtain a bit and we saw my uncle, Father's younger brother, who was then about 20. He was a very handsome young man, with blue eyes, well-built and muscular, a lock of hair curling across his forehead. He hardly looked Jewish at all. He wore a light-colored trench coat, in the fashion of the local young gentiles. Jewish young men in our town usually wore dark clothes and always wore a hat in public. To our surprise, my uncle was bareheaded and was also without the yellow patch.

My father signaled my uncle to enter through the window, which he opened for him, so as not to tamper with the wax seal on the door. Menachem climbed easily through the window and with a quick leap landed on the floor in the room. We all gathered around him affectionately, and after we calmed down a bit he told us about what had happened to all our many relatives. While we were in the attic, everyone in his large family, but him, had been sent on the last transport, including two uncles with their small children. The two older sons of my uncle Avraham had fled into the hills, to join the partisans. Menachem had come to say farewell to us before following them.

Barely ten minutes had passed—the adults were talking in a whisper and we girls were listening to every word—when we heard the lock turn. Then the door burst open and two policemen entered. We froze in horror. I thought, this was the end! What a pity we went through that hard time in the attic, now our end has come anyway, and look how stupidly we were caught, and it was mostly our fault, too, for leaving a relatively safe shelter.

We were ordered to take a bit of food and clothing, but there was little to take, because we had left everything in the attic. We were led out of the apartment by the *gardists*, who re-sealed the door behind us. We walked with my uncle in silence, passing through the familiar streets, now totally deserted. On the way others joined us, some of them whole families who had been found in their hiding places and looked as frightened as we did.

Father whispered to himself, "It's so symbolic! Today is Tisha b'Av, and maybe our destruction is near. Where are they taking us, what is going to happen? Is this the end of our hiding?"

A shudder ran through me as I listened to Father's mumbling. I held fast to the hand of my sister Rachel. Father carried little Miriam, and so we marched, the policemen hurrying us to our prison. We knew there was no way back; we would all be sent to where the others had already gone.

"So that's what happened, Grandma? You were taken on a train like all the others I saw in the photographs and heard about on Holocaust Memorial Day? But how were you rescued?," my granddaughter Omer asks in a muted voice, tears welling up in her heavy-lidded eyes.

"Just wait, our ordeal was a long way from over," I said. "Even after we were caught, things went unexpectedly. And in the next chapter you will get an answer to your question."

Shout, Little Girl

Other Jews who had also been caught joined our procession. Escorted by two armed guards, we neared the high school where those who were rounded up were taken. There was an oppressive silence. Outside the building, there was a large courtyard with an iron gate in the center. We saw women, men, children, infants and old people, too, sitting or lying on the ground in small groups in the middle of the courtyard.

I noticed something strange. A few people were lying on stretchers with the symbol of the hospital and the Red Cross. I couldn't take my eyes off the stretchers. My heart skipped a beat and I was gripped with foreboding. What were these people doing here? Why had they been taken even though they were ill? I felt unsteady, as though I was in a nightmare. I asked my parents whether these people, too, were going to be sent to "work." Had the doctors agreed to let the patients be taken from the hospital? What could they possibly "contribute to the war effort"? Something strange and very bad was going on! Ominous suspicions began to assail me. The sight of the people on the stretchers, some of whom were groaning quietly, made me shudder. I started to shake all over. Father looked at me sadly and turned his gaze, not answering my questions. In Mother's eyes I saw distress and helplessness.

We later learned that the sick and elderly people had indeed been removed from the hospitals where they were being treated. The mentally ill Jews in the closed ward were also taken. These wretched human beings were added to the few who were caught hiding, like us, or whose permit to remain in the town had expired. It was one of the last transports.

In a state of shock, I sat with my family by the others. I stared at the hospital patients with dull, dry eyes. Our daring attempt to escape our fate was over, I thought. All we could do was wait. No one spoke a word. Our minds, too, were empty. All I wanted to do was go to sleep and forget the reality around me.

Then I heard some sort of muttering on my right. I turned toward the sound and saw a beautiful girl of about 18 lying on a stretcher. She was staring at the sky, expressionless. Her mother sat on the ground next to her, holding her hand. Suddenly the girl sat up and began to sway back and forth, muttering, in Hungarian, "*Legy boldog*" ("Be happy"). She repeated the words over and over, sometimes lying down and then sitting up again.

Her mother caressed her light hair and her forehead, and occasionally moistened her dry lips. A few minutes later the girl stopped swaying, lay down silently and cast her vacant gaze on some unseen object. Then, after a time, the scene played itself out again, like some sort of prayer or ritual. I watched her, almost hypnotized. I saw no one but her. I waited for her to repeat the words. I couldn't take my eyes off her beautiful but frightening face. Around me, people whispered that the girl had gone out of her mind, because she couldn't bear the anguish of departing from her sisters and her girlfriends, who had been taken on earlier transports.

I felt suffocated and nauseous. My stomach seemed to be shriveling up and a sharp pain pierced my lower body. The pain came in waves, like birth pangs. At first I groaned with soft sobs, but when the pain intensified I started to moan and groan aloud, without shame, as though all the rules of behavior I had been taught no longer existed.

Mother sat by me as though paralyzed, clasping her hands helplessly, not knowing what to do. Then an acquaintance of ours came over to me and asked where the pain was, exactly. I pointed to a spot in my stomach, all the while crying, and she said without the slightest hesitation, "Aliska, put your hand on the right side of your stomach and shout stronger, with all your might!" Then she turned to one of the guards and said, "Look at this poor girl... She is writhing with pain... It must be her appendix... You can't send her on this transport in her condition! She needs to see a doctor right away."

Taking his cue from the woman, Father asked the guards to let him take me to a nearby hospital. The guards whispered among themselves and then gave their consent. "Take the girl and run to a doctor. Only try to get back before the transport leaves!"

Father leaped to his feet and picked me up. I went on crying with pain, as the gate opened and Father ran toward the hospital, carrying me in his arms.

Again we were outside and free! Out of the corner of my eye, I saw everyone watching us. And then, miraculously, we met my uncle Menachem, who had been detained with us, walking casually along the street—not running—pretending to be calm and safe. Afterward we learned that he had escaped through an opening in the courtyard. He forced himself not to look at us, only giving us a wink to show we shouldn't speak to him and should act as though he were a total stranger.

I felt we had been saved. I wanted to shout with happiness but I still didn't know how things would turn out. Father carried me like a fragile package, holding me in front of him with his arms stretched out. Soon he started breathing more heavily and he ran more slowly. At the hospital, Father let me down carefully. Then something strange happened: the pain disappeared completely and I stood there, feet firmly on the ground, smiling, and said, "Father, it doesn't hurt anymore. Can we go back to Mother now?" To my surprise, I saw a mixture of fear and pleading in my Father's eyes. "My little girl," he whispered to me, "please, don't stand so upright! Keep on twisting and pretend that you are suffering and crying—otherwise, we are lost! They will send us straight back to that courtyard and we will be deported with them all this very day."

But Father, what about Mother and the girls?" I replied angrily. But he went on: "Everything will be fine, just don't stop moaning and complaining."

And he picked me up again and started walking toward the main building of the hospital complex.

Inside the gate we were directed to an office in the front of the building. I was admitted to the examining room. Again I was seized with fear and the pains came back, though not as sharply as before. We were received by a Jewish doctor whom Father knew, and this seemed to hearten him and give him hope.

After listening to my father's story about what happened, the doctor told me to lie down and started to examine my stomach, pressing it all over. When he asked where it hurt me, I told him "everywhere," because the truth was that it didn't hurt me anywhere. The doctor suddenly stopped examining me, looked through his glasses straight into Father's eyes, and said, "The girl has no medical problem. The pains were probably due to the fear she felt in the schoolyard. I will be risking my freedom if I admit her here without a valid reason. But what I will do is transfer her to the director of the department, Dr. Bullock. He is a Czech doctor and not a bad man, and fortunately for you, he is very greedy. If you can 'grease his palm,' he might agree to hospitalize the girl until after this transport leaves."

Father shook the doctor's hand gratefully, but showed no signs of happiness. His eyes betrayed bewilderment and concern for Mother and the girls, who were still in detention. I asked him again, directly, "And what about Mother and the girls?" He tried to calm me and said, in his usual way, "Shhh... shhh... Everything will be all right, little girl. After you are in the hospital, I will get permits for their release."

As we were talking, a nun who was a hospital nurse came

in and placed me on a stretcher. I was taken to another room, where five women of different ages were lying. They looked at me curiously, and I didn't know how to behave. Should I cry or keep quiet? Father told me, "Lie quietly, I am going out for a minute." I felt terribly alone and I was afraid that Father would not come back and I would never see him again. But less than ten minutes later he returned with Mother and the girls. I raised myself on my elbows, in disbelief. I was sure I was having delusions. After all, Mother was in detention with all the Jews! But no, this was real.

Mother told me that after we left she began to cry hysterically and begged to be allowed to go with her little girl to the hospital, because maybe Aliska would die and she wouldn't have a chance to say a final goodbye. She cried and screamed, and said her two little girls would stay behind until she returned, so it was certain that she would come back after seeing me alive, because obviously she was not going to abandon her two little ones. After this very persuasive reasoning was translated by other detainees, the guards let her go.

But as soon as the gate opened, Rachel grabbed the hand of her sister Miriam and both of them started crying and running after Mother. The guards seemed to be stunned at this sudden turn of events, but for some reason they did not stop them from leaving. Then, when the three of them were outside, they all began to run like mad to the hospital.

At the hospital, they met Father, who was wandering around the courtyard in a daze, trying to figure out a solution to our problem. Delighted and overwhelmed at seeing them, Father took Mother and my sisters to my room, but after we all embraced and broke out in tears, to release our emotions, they were ordered to leave. And despite this temporary "victory," there were still quite a few questions to be answered: Would Father be able to persuade the head of the department to hospitalize me, and where would he get the money? Where would the others go if the hospital agreed to keep me, and what would happen then? And how and where would they spend the night, and what would happen tomorrow morning?

*"Grandma, why didn't they go straight to your apartment?"
Omer asked, logically.*

"Do you remember how I told you that when the gardists took us from our home, they locked the door and placed an official seal of the authorities on it, which meant that the apartment became 'government property'? No one was allowed to enter the apartment, certainly not anyone from our family, some of whom had cleverly escaped from the transport. There was no chance of staying in the apartment without being discovered. We would only have been caught again."

Not satisfied with my answer, Omer went on pressing me: "So what happened to them? Where did they spend the night?"

"Mother and the girls found themselves in a situation where they had only two possibilities: to spend the night in the hospital garden—which, fortunately, was possible in the summer weather; or to sneak back into the apartment despite everything and hide there until morning. I will tell you right away what they decided to do."

The Operation

True, I was in the hospital, but I was free. And not only me — my whole family was free. Before Mother and Father left my room in the surgical ward, I heard them talking about where they would go and where they would spend the night. Father hinted that there was only one reasonable place: our apartment. They would be able to enter through the window, like last time, and stay there for the night, he said. If everything went well, they would return to the hospital early in the morning and then try to find a more permanent hiding place.

But Mother was against this plan; she was very much afraid, and with good reason. She believed that after their dramatic escape from the transport, the first place the authorities would look for her and my sisters was in our apartment. Father accepted this argument, and so, having no other choice, they spent the night in the hospital garden, sleeping on benches. Actually, only the girls slept — Mother and Father didn't get a wink of sleep all night. Even though it was July, the night was quite chilly, and they were wearing only light summer clothes. On top of this, the lights in the garden were on all night, and

Mother and Father were afraid they would be chased away at any moment.

Late at night, Father stole into our courtyard to see what was going on there. Most of the apartments were empty by now and the courtyard was almost deserted. There were only two families there: the landlord's family, who were exempted from deportation, and a non-Jewish family, who had "inherited" one of the apartments as a reward for its loyalty to the fascist party.

Father knocked on the landlord's door. The man was stunned to see him—after all, we had been taken for transport the day before! After listening to the story, the landlord advised Father to leave immediately and not endanger himself. After they parted, Father hid behind a tree in the courtyard and watched our apartment. During the time he was there, until midnight, no one entered or left the flat, and nothing suspicious took place. As he made his way back to the hospital, Father decided that, despite the danger, they would spend the coming nights in the apartment, as he had planned.

In the meantime, yours truly, the heroine of the episode, was lying in a bed between clean sheets, refusing to comprehend what was going on around her. From sheer exhaustion, I fell into a deep sleep. When I awoke the next morning, Father was by my bedside and he whispered to me that Mother was with the girls in the garden and that the night had passed quietly. He had learned from a neighbor that those being sent on the transport had already been taken to the train station and would probably leave for the East within a few hours. As long as they agreed to keep me in the hospital, Father said, we were safe. Naturally, a great deal depended on my ability to pretend I was ill. Father's words made me uneasy and I had another panic attack and started to cry. Father tried to comfort me. He said he was confident I could play my part well, and asked only that I rest comfortably.

But I was a bundle of nerves. I kept casting suspicious glances at the other patients in the room, and I was terribly afraid about how things would turn out. Father told me how to behave when the head doctor came on his rounds: when he examined me, I was to say that I had severe pains on the right side of my stomach, where the appendix was located. But I didn't care for the idea of having to pretend again that I was sick. I was afraid that I wouldn't be able to lie convincingly and fool a skilled doctor, when actually I felt no pain at all. Father begged me and said it was our only chance to escape the deportation, which was now so close. I imagine that Father already knew that the transport was not just for "work."

The critical moment soon arrived. The doctor, wearing a white robe, entered the room together with a nurse, who was a nun and wore a broad-brimmed hat. I looked carefully at the doctor. I had hoped he would be a sympathetic person. What I saw was a squat man with a round, bald head and a red face; he looked more like the owner of a butcher shop than a doctor. He examined the women in the room one after the other, and when he got to me, he looked at the card that was attached to the end of the bed and said, "Well, little girl, do you still have pains?"

I looked at him but I couldn't get a word out. I nodded

my head to indicate that I was still in pain.

Father stood next to me, tense and restless. The doctor introduced himself, even though they had already met, as it was only with his consent that I had been hospitalized, after he heard about my case from the Jewish doctor.

"I am Dr. Bullock, the director of the ward," he said. "Let's see what is happening with the girl." He aggressively lifted the blanket, pulled up the white hospital dressing gown, and began examining my stomach. Every time he pressed, he asked me whether it hurt. I wasn't sure where it was supposed to hurt exactly, so most times I answered, "Yes, it hurts here and also here."

The doctor looked at me as though to say, Whom do you think you are trying to fool? Then he covered me with the blanket and said to Father with a wink, "Fine, we will see what we can do. In the meantime she will remain here in the hospital. You must come to my office."

Father's eyes lit up. I saw a new glimmer of hope in them. My heart started pounding strangely, from total happiness: Did that mean I would be able to stay in this clean bed and get good food, too? Maybe everything would work out after all? It must be a gift from God! After the doctor had finished examining the patients, Father went to his office. I couldn't wait for him to come back. He returned a short time later and told me what had happened. Dr. Bullock had told him that he knew for a fact that I was completely healthy, but in return for payment—quite a lot of money—he would agree to leave me in the hospital, even though by doing so he was taking a grave personal risk. I knew Father didn't have enough money to pay for the doctor's "favor" and I felt another sharp pain in my stomach, which this time was a sign of anxiety.

"What will be, Father?" I asked.

He turned away, looked out the window, and said, "We'll see, I'll come up with something, I'll think of who we can turn to."

I remembered suddenly that I hadn't seen Mother since the day before and that I needed her now more than ever, even if she could not calm my fears. I asked Father where she and the girls were and he bent over and whispered, "They are in the garden here. I bring them food. During the day they will be here, near you. Mother will come to see you soon for a bit, and toward evening we will go home to sleep."

I spent most of the day sleeping. The dramatic events and my effort not to break down and to go on playing the sick heroine must have exhausted me. I was weak, tired, and drowsy. I didn't wake up until the food was brought in. I sat up and poked at the meal listlessly, without any appetite. I only ate a little and I hid the rest under the blanket. When Father came back for another visit I gave him the food for the family and he quickly put it into his pockets, without anyone noticing. He told me that Mother and the girls were waiting in the garden and didn't dare show themselves to the hospital staff.

I was anxious and worried about what would happen, and I felt very much alone. How would our new "adventure" end? It was such a heavy responsibility for a girl my age that it made me very nervous, and inside I was shaking all the time. I longed for my Mother; I needed her so much at this time when everything was so uncertain and the mental pressure did not stop. I longed for her touch and for her words of cheer; all I wanted to do was cling to her and cry on her bosom, like I did when I was a little girl.

On his afternoon rounds, Dr. Bullock again came over to my bed and asked, "Where is your father, that *feshak?*" The word he used was Czech for "a good fellow," but to me it sounded like *veshak*, which reminded me of the word for "hanging", and it scared me very much. "He promised to bring the payment, what is delaying him?" I thought he meant that Father should be hanged for not bringing the money.

I started to stammer that Father was probably on the way. The poor man must be running around trying to raise the money, I thought to myself, and he must be having a hard time.

"I believe you have recovered," the doctor said assertively, "and that it will be possible to send you home today."

Home? What home was he talking about, where did I have a home? Before he could leave, I grabbed his hand. It was an extraordinarily daring thing to do for me. I begged and cried, "Please, doctor, don't send me—you know exactly what that means. Father will certainly bring you the payment soon."

Looking at his fat, flushed face, I felt a strong repulsion. I was still holding onto his hand, but I felt my strength fading and I weakened my grip. After a short hesitation he pulled his hand away and said in a friendlier tone, "What, all right, then, tomorrow we are operating on you. Just tell your father he has to honor his commitment."

After the doctor left I felt a sense of relief and an inexplicable wild happiness. Then, suddenly, I grasped what the doctor had said — that they were going to operate on me tomorrow. What does that mean? I thought to myself. How much will it hurt, and what will the operation mean for my future life? I didn't know a thing about the operation or what they would do to me. After all, everyone knew I wasn't really sick, so why this frightening and unnecessary operation? Still, it was good that I would be able to stay in the hospital — it was so safe here compared to the terrible dangers outside.

Later, when Father returned, I told him the news. I also told him about how angry the doctor had been. He gave me a warm hug and his eyes sparkled from happiness. Then he calmed me down by telling me he already had most of the money and that he was going to give it to the doctor immediately. Finally he patted my head gently and said, "You are brave and good, my little girl. Now we will be able to stay here at least a week, maybe even two weeks, until you recover completely from the operation. I hope that in the meantime we all find salvation."

Even today, over 50 years later, I am still thrilled and amazed at Father's inexhaustible optimism, even when everything around seemed to be falling apart. He gave me a grateful look with his warm, innocent eyes. Even through his thick glasses I could see that his eyes were moist.

The preparations for the operation were made the evening before. I was alone, a girl of 12, and I couldn't understand the instructions of the anesthetist, who explained what would happen. He promised me I wouldn't feel anything, I would be under full anesthesia and would sleep right through the operation. He avoided answering my question about what exactly they were going to do, saying only, "Don't be afraid, everything will be fine. Dr. Bullock is an excellent surgeon."

Still, I was afraid of what lay in store and felt terrible stress: fear of the operation and resentment toward my parents for consenting to such a radical and perhaps even dangerous step so that we could stay put. Was there a chance that we would be saved after I recovered from the unnecessary operation? And what if I died during surgery? I remembered stories about unsuccessful operations that ended with the patient dying or becoming a cripple. I was very tense and cried all the time until I finally fell asleep.

The truth is that it is not only difficult but almost impossible today to explain the situation I was in. We had been bitterly persecuted and faced a concrete threat of deportation and death. When people, even small children, find themselves in an extraordinary situation, they discover the power to do extraordinary things, which the human mind cannot grasp or describe. We have tremendous hidden powers that suddenly appear and make it possible for us to survive in a time of trial. And sometimes we do daring deeds, for which we can find no rational explanation afterward.

I remember only bits and pieces from the operation. Two nuns moved me from my bed onto a high stretcher and I was wheeled through endless corridors to the operating room, which was shiningly clean and white. The bright lights above dazzled me. A mask was placed on my nose, and through it they pumped an anesthetic that had a bad smell and made me feel light-headed. To this day, whenever I go by a gas station, the smell reminds me of the narcotic in the operation. The anesthetist told me to count, and I guess I was fast asleep within a few seconds.

When I woke up, I hazily saw Father sitting by me in the recovery room. At first everything was blurred. On the small cupboard next to my bed stood a vase with flowers; I have no idea where they came from. When I moved I felt a strong pain shoot through my stomach. I touched the place that hurt and discovered that it was thickly wrapped in bandages. I groaned and wanted to tell Father I was thirsty, but I couldn't, because my mouth was dry and blocked with a tube that was stuck into my burning throat.

I was desperate for something to drink, and when I signaled Father to come over to the bed, I saw that tears were flowing from his eyes. I was so moved by this that I almost forgot the pain and the thirst. Father was crying! My father was crying and muttering, "My poor little girl, you are suffering this needless pain for all of us, you are our saving angel." I asked for something to drink, but Father bent over close to me and explained that the doctors said I couldn't have anything to drink after the operation, but could only wet my lips.

Suddenly, as though possessed by a demon, I grabbed the vase, threw away the flowers, and was about to drink the putrid water. At the last second, Father stopped me. I lashed out at him wildly with my weak arms and gasped, "You made me suffer all this, so at least let me drink!" Father looked at me pityingly and wept silently. I can still clearly see him crying and hear his choking voice. I am so overwhelmed by this, even all these years later, that I shudder all over when I think of it. I was given a sedative and fell asleep.

When I awoke, I saw Father sitting next to me, dozing. I felt better. I asked why Mother did not visit me. Father reassured me, saying that Mother was still hiding in the garden with the girls and was afraid to enter the hospital because she thought the hospital staff might turn her over to the authorities. Only Father had permission to stay with me, and he remained by my bed for the first two days after the operation, strengthening my spirit. But I missed Mother's presence and my heart longed for her. Here I was after an operation that had no medical cause, and she was not with me at this trying time.

I don't remember what happened in the days that followed, except that Mother could not resist the temptation and came to visit me a few times, despite the danger. She was pale and agitated, and looked thinner. Tension and anxiety were clearly written on her face. I remember one visit, when the anguish she was going through contorted her face with grief and suffering. The kerchief on her head had partly slipped off, her clothes were rumpled, and all she did was stand next to my bed and cry continuously and helplessly. After that, Father and Mother took turns staying with me.

My temperature, which was taken every day, gradually fell. Twice a day the nurse-nun would stick a thermometer under my armpit and then go to check other patients. We knew that when my temperature returned to normal, I would have to leave the hospital. So Mother decided to trick the nurse. While she did her rounds, Mother rubbed the thermometer between her fingers until it rose to at least 38 degrees Celsius (100.4 degrees Fahrenheit), and then put it back under my armpit. When the nurse returned to check the thermometer, she would enter the reading on my personal card with the note, "Temperature not down yet."

So my recovery from the operation took longer than usual, but I have very few memories of the days I spent in the hospital. There is one embarrassing event that I do remember clearly, because it was so terrifying.

On that day, the nurse came in and gave out the thermometers, as usual. As soon as she turned her back on us, Mother took it and rubbed it until the mercury inside had risen to the temperature she wanted. Then she put it back.

This time, when the nurse returned, she looked carefully at the thermometer, then at us, and back at the thermometer again. Suddenly she put her hand on my forehead, and without a word, shook the thermometer until it reached its starting point. She then placed it under my armpit and stood there, waiting. Right away, I knew the game was up and that we were in big trouble. I was paralyzed with fear. Surely the nurse and the other patients in the room could hear my heart pounding. It was beating so loud, as though it were about to burst. The insides of my stomach seemed to heave, I became hot all over, and my head sank heavily onto the pillow. I was trembling all over and suddenly felt as though I were freezing.

The seconds ticked by slowly, until finally the nurse glanced at her watch and decided that enough time had passed. She took out the thermometer and as she looked at it I saw the amazement in her eyes. I heard her mumble to herself, "Interesting, she has a fever after all—not as high as before, but still over 38 degrees." She recorded the temperature on the card and left without saying another word.

Because of the other patients in the room, I had to restrain myself from shouting with joy. If our trick had been discovered, we would all have been thrown out of the hospital at once and sent straight to arrest and detention. Now we had gained more time to stay in the hospital. Mother and I knew that a great miracle had happened and that we had been saved from being sent on a transport at the last minute. And this was not the last miracle we were to experience during the long years of the war.

In the meantime, Father managed to raise the rest of the money for the surgeon, who, in return ordered that I be kept in the hospital for twice as long as was needed—until one day he informed us that I could stay there no longer and would have to leave. During the last examination before I left the hospital, the doctor placed an especially large bandage on the place where the incision was made—actually, it had already healed completely—and we went back to our apartment.

We had barely organized ourselves in the apartment when, that very day, two *gardists* appeared and ordered us to accompany them. I lay in bed, even though I could easily walk. "The girl is sick," Mother told the two policemen, and Father added, "She has just come through a serious operation."

"See for yourselves," Mother said, lifting my nightgown, to my great embarrassment. "The wound is still fresh under the bandage."

"She just came back from the hospital today," Father went on. "We have all the papers."

For a moment I thought the brutal policemen were going to rip off the bandage and see that the wound had healed. Fortunately, they believed the story, but told us in no uncertain terms that the moment the doctor said I was healthy, we were to report immediately for the next transport. Later we learned that a few other women had also undergone fake operations—in return for generous payment, of course—but no girls of my age. Whenever the subject came up, my parents were always proud of me, and grateful for the rest of their lives.

The anti-Jewish orders were issued by the departments in charge of "solving the Jewish question." However, a few days later, Mother learned that, at the initiative of the President of the independent Slovak Republic, Dr. Tiso, who was a Catholic priest, a law had been passed under which Jews who converted to Christianity and had a certificate to prove it bearing an appropriate date, were exempt from deportation.

Mother worked feverishly to get the document, which was known as the "*shmad-tsetel*" (conversion certificate), but without Father's knowledge. She and other Jews rushed around trying to make contact with clergymen who would be willing to issue the coveted authorization. She knew that what she was doing was a betrayal of the Jewish tradition, and that "death was to be preferred" to the use of such a document. In fact, the majority of the Jews in the town did not convert or even pretend to convert during the entire period of the deportations. But in order to save us, under the precept of *pikuah nefesh*, "saving an endangered life" (as she interpreted it), Mother ignored the prohibition.

She decided that she had to obtain the necessary certificates, come what may, and in any way possible. It was very difficult to find clergymen who were bold enough to issue conversion certificates dated four years back. If caught, they could be severely punished, as they were forbidden to turn Jews into "new Christians." Fortunately, with the help of a gentile woman friend, Mother was put in touch with a Protestant priest, who was one of the few who opposed the fascist regime and was ready to help those who turned to him. He was critical of the church's indifference and was ashamed of its institutions, which frequently collaborated in the persecution of the Jews.

Mother went to see him and he gave her the certificate. Many others obtained such documents in return for payment. It was difficult to get a certificate from Catholic priests, many of whom were among the leaders and activists of the ruling party, which was highly anti-Semitic. The priests who risked their lives and helped the Jews were Protestants and Lutherans, who themselves suffered persecution at the hands of the fascists, or Russian Orthodox and Greek Orthodox. However, the freedom we gained with the help of the fake document did not last long, and soon we had to come up with a new solution.

The Refugee Camp

It was 1943. In half a year I would be 13, and maybe a student in sixth grade, too. By some miracle, things had calmed down a little, even though the year had begun with a threat by the Minister of the Interior that in March, or April at the latest, the transports would start again. However, this did not happen, probably because of the Germans' first defeats on the Eastern Front. The Russians had the upper hand, but the Germans did not surrender and their retreat proceeded slowly.

The reports from the Russian front were an elixir of life for the surviving Jews in Eastern Slovakia. The atmosphere became more encouraging. The partisans also stepped up their activity and announced that the Russians were advancing. However, the authorities again found a scapegoat in the form of the Jews, whom they now accused of aiding the partisans. Anyone caught helping them would be severely punished. At the same time, the impression was that the Slovak fascists wanted to prove their tolerance and their sympathy for the persecuted. They made no special effort to liquidate the few remaining Jews—perhaps they wanted an alibi for when the day of reckoning arrived.

So the few children who still remained in the town after all the deportations returned to school. Teachers who had been in hiding emerged and joined those who had immunity from deportation, and together they organized matters and gathered the remaining pupils. We continued going to school as though the ground was not burning beneath our feet, as though there was no war and the Jews were not being sent away to unknown destinations. School was still safer territory than home, and far safer than the street. Never was anyone taken from school for deportation with his family. Still, our school was a gauge for the scale of the calamity: where once there were 700 pupils aged 6 to 16, there were now barely 60.

In the autumn of 1943, we learned that a few residents of our town had escaped from concentration camps around Lublin, in Poland, and had made their way back to Michalovce by a tortuous route, traveling through forests while on the brink of starvation. They told in detail about the atrocities that were being perpetrated against the Jews, especially children, women, and the elderly—by then the Nazis' extermination machine was working at full intensity—but the stories were only whispered. True, efforts were made to make the truth known and rouse the world, but those in the international community who should have known and taken action bided their time. A foul atmosphere descended on our town and the old fears came back—and things were only made worse because we had already begun to believe that everyone who had survived until now was basically safe. As the threats about more deportations grew, people again started trying to cross the

Hungarian border. The Hungarians had not yet touched the Jews, apart from recruiting males of army age, who were sent to forced-labor camps instead of doing military service.

Mother and Father decided that we girls should be sent to Hungary again, to our Aunt Mariska and Uncle Jeno in Budapest. They got in touch with someone who smuggled people across the border and decided to send the three of us with him. Using the same method as the previous time—a special code together with Hebrew words in otherwise innocent letters—Mother and Father let our relatives know we would be arriving. But the village that was chosen for the border crossing was not the same one as on that first failed attempt.

It was early December. We were given warm clothes and fur-lined boots for the long trek; more clothes were packed in a small bag. Toward evening we parted quickly, so as not to draw out the grief and to prevent any last-minute regrets. We set out for the train station with the smuggler all alone, without Mother and Father, who were afraid that a large group might attract attention and endanger the plan.

The train was already at the station when we got there. The engine puffed white smoke into the sky. We followed the man into one of the cars and soon were on our way. Memories of the failed attempt last time made me uneasy and I prayed in my heart that we would succeed. Surprisingly, the journey was very short. The man signaled to us to follow him. I took my sisters' hands as we got off at the last station before the border. It was already dark, the station was almost completely deserted, and no one paid any attention to us. Right away we made our way to an open field in front of us. The man took little Miriam on his back like a sack of potatoes. She placed her head on his shoulder and cuddled up to him. He told Rachel and me to stay close to him and not say a word, so that we could get by the border police.

There was snow on the ground and every step we took left footprints. We walked through an empty, treeless field; a dark sky hung low over us and the horizon was empty. We saw no paths or any other signs of a trail. Everything looked the same, an endless plain with no landmarks. I was amazed: how did the man know whether he should go left, right, or straight ahead? But he walked ahead confidently — he must know the way well from all his missions in the past. In one hand he held a bag and on his back was a little girl. Every once in a while he lowered Miriam, rested a few minutes, and then swung her back onto his broad shoulders.

We walked for a long time, maybe a few hours. I felt very tired and was finding it harder and harder to keep up such a fast pace in the snow. My whole body was freezing cold, especially my face and feet. I kept thinking about how things had gone wrong with the peasant woman who had imprisoned us in that church steeple below the horrible bell, and about the bitter disappointment then. Anxiety that the same thing would happen again almost paralyzed me and made me shiver inside, as if the cold wasn't enough.

I don't know how long our night trek lasted. Finally, we saw lights in the distance. Cheerfully, the man told us, "Girls, we are already in Hungary. We crossed the border safely and we will soon come to a train station."

I was astonished, as I had expected barbed-wire fences or armed guards. Instead, we had come through a deserted place where everything looked the same and there was total silence.

We aroused no suspicion in the train station. We all spoke excellent Hungarian. After a few stations, we reached the town where the smuggler was to hand over the "package" to relatives of ours, who would later take us to Budapest. The man asked for directions to the address my parents had given him, and late that same night we arrived at the home of our relatives, that were awaiting our arrival.

A pleasant warmth enveloped us in the house. It made us very sleepy, and we almost collapsed on the spot. It was very late and we had had a long, exhausting day. I couldn't wait any longer and lay down on the floor, completely drained, and my sisters did the same. All we wanted to do was sleep.

The family—parents and two small children—gathered around us with curiosity. They helped us up, sat us down on a sofa, and gave us apple juice. After we recovered a bit, they introduced themselves and asked us to do the same and tell them how old we were. The parents told us that we were second cousins and that they had once visited us, long ago. Our "deliverer" showed them Father's letter. He was given something to eat and drink, and then left immediately, taking with him a letter from our Hungarian cousins stating that we had arrived safely. Our relatives took our coats and our wet boots, and they hugged and kissed us, lamenting our sad fate. Like many Hungarian Jews, they were certain that they were in no danger. After all, their families had been Hungarian citizens for generations and they were loyal to their country; the non-Jewish citizens would surely not allow "their" Jews to suffer as we had. After we washed and had a snack, we went to bed and fell asleep instantly.

The next morning the mother of the family took us to the capital, Budapest. The trip took several hours. I was amazed and thrilled by the huge, fancy train station in Budapest. I was fascinated by the constant bustle as streams of people came and went. We were in one of the most beautiful cities in Central Europe, and as a girl who had come from a town of 15,000, I was absolutely dazzled.

We made our way through the streets to the tram that would take us to the home of our aunt and uncle. I couldn't take my eyes off the tall buildings and I was entranced by all the cars, trams and carriages that drove along the wide boulevards. The streets were crowded with people, and they all seemed to be in a hurry. I looked at the shop windows, and, despite the cold, I asked if we could stop from time to time, so I could get a good look at the displays.

Then we boarded the tram. It was my first trip on a tram, and I enjoyed it very much. We came to a six-story building. I had never seen such a tall building—the highest building in our town was only three stories. We walked up the stairs to the second floor and rang the bell. The door opened and there stood my Aunt Mariska and Uncle Jeno, who were very moved to see us, with their three small children, a boy, Simon, and two girls, Györgyi and Vali. I tried to match their faces to the photographs I had seen of them, and waited expectantly to see what kind of welcome we would get. We rushed in, they embraced and kissed us over and over, and all our feelings were released in emotional tears. Thank God, we had arrived safely. After the many ordeals of the journey, I felt I had reached a safe haven, my new home.

The relative who had brought us stayed a few hours and then left, with the promise that we would meet again. But, in fact, we never saw her again: She and her family perished, along with most of Hungarian Jewry.

When we had calmed down a little, the questions came thick and fast. At first I felt confused and bewildered, as though I were on the witness stand in court and had to defend myself. Quickly, though, I became very emotional as the memories began to flood over me. I told about Mother and Father, about the situation at home, the plunder, the humilliations, the transports, the persecution — and, of course, about my fake operation. But I had the feeling that they didn't believe me, that they thought I had a wild imagination and was making up most of what I told them. After all, none of this could really have happened, not in enlightened Europe.

The writing was on the wall in Hungary, too, but people refused to pay attention to the danger signs. As long as there were no deportations, Hungarian Jews lived quite securely and were relatively well-off. Hungary was the only country in Nazi-occupied Europe where the Jews had not yet been persecuted. It was all an illusion, of course, but it gave people a false sense of security.

Our happiness at being able to live safely in our new

home proved premature. For the time being, we would have to leave, my uncle explained, because under the law it was forbidden to take in refugee children; both those who were illegally in the country and those who gave them shelter would be punished severely if caught. Our best hope was to enter a refugee camp that housed persecuted children from countries such as Slovakia, Poland, and Serbia. The camp was classified as an orphanage, *Szabolcs*, and under the law, children from the camp could be adopted by Hungarian citizens, though this was done mainly by Jewish families. The plan was for Uncle Jeno to take us to the camp, where we would tell the authorities that we had escaped by ourselves from Slovakia with the help of good people and that we wanted shelter.

So the next morning we packed our few clothes and our aunt gave us food for the journey. After another delightful ride on the tram, we reached the camp. Our uncle left and we approached the gate, three frightened girls. But to our surprise, no one stopped us or asked us any questions, and we were immediately given beds in a small room with four girls from Serbia. They looked at us suspiciously but quickly became friendly and pleasant. Using body language only, they told us they were happy that we were joining them. They, themselves, had met by chance in the camp and since then had always stayed together. Their problem was that they didn't know Hungarian. I understood a little of what they said—Slovakian and Serbian are both Slavic languages, so some words are similar—and I interpreted for them until they learned the words and phrases they needed for everyday matters.

In time, I became friends with one of them, a girl about my age who impressed me with her beautiful singing, because I liked to sing, too. She would sing and hum to herself, mostly melancholy tunes, while staring into space as though sending a secret message to those who had been left behind. When she sang, other children came to listen, too. She had a clear, high voice, like a bird, and her singing made me feel an inexplicable longing and sadness. She taught me songs in Serbian and we sang them together.

We stayed in the camp about six weeks, spending the time mostly eating and playing group games. Every day we waited for our relatives to visit. We would meander around the yard and look through the fence, only to return disappointed when they did not come. When they visited, we hoped we would soon be able to leave, most of all because we couldn't move around freely in the camp. Every day we watched enviously as happy children left with their adoptive families. We also met new children who arrived after being caught trying to get across the border, or who came to the camp on their own.

On one of their visits, my aunt and uncle brought us a wonderful surprise: a letter from Mother and Father. This was a great event, because the postal services between countries had all but broken down. We ran our fingers over the letter lovingly and longingly, and kissed the pages, as though that would reunite us with our parents.

Mother and Father wrote that they were very happy that all had gone well, that a great weight had been lifted from their heart and that they were grateful to God for the knowledge that we were safe. So as not to make things hard for our relatives, they suggested that we split up. Once we were out of the camp, Rachel, the middle sister, would go to our grandparents' place in the country, where Grandfather was a religious court judge and ritual slaughterer, and provided religious services to the surrounding villages. Rachel was upset at this, but our Aunt Mariska promised her that she would like the place and would be spoiled silly, and that it would make our grandparents happy if she came to live with them. But then Rachel fell ill in the refugee camp, as though fate wanted to delay her painful departure. The doctors said she had to have an emergency operation to remove her tonsils, which were constantly becoming inflamed. The poor girl cried a lot, not only because of the physical pain, but mostly because she would have to go through the operation by herself, far from Mother and Father, in a strange land. At first she refused to go to the village and live with our grandmother and grandfather, but it had all been worked out between the adults and finally she agreed to go.

A few weeks later, the adoption was authorized and we returned to the large and beautiful flat of our aunt and uncle. Uncle Jeno took my sister — who had recovered from the operation — to the village, where our grandmother and grandfather, and also a maiden aunt, Ilonka, were waiting for her. My little sister stayed with me in Budapest. After a few days, we felt as though it was our home. Miriam played with her cousins, who were a bit younger than she was, and I, as the oldest, watched over them.

After some time had passed, my aunt noticed that I had sores on the back of my neck and was scratching them all the time. When another relative, who was a doctor, came to visit, she asked him to have a look. It didn't take long before he said, "The girl's hair is crawling with lice, and they are causing the sores. Her hair is full of them and she has probably infected the other girls, too."

Aunt Mariska examined everyone thoroughly and was appalled to see that we all had lice and lice eggs. In those days, kerosene or cabbage juice was used to remove the nasty insects. The liquid was smeared into our hair and our heads were wrapped in a towel for a few hours, and then the lice were removed with the aid of a special comb. A piece of white paper was placed under us, so it would be easy to spot and destroy the insects when they fell. I felt ashamed. I knew the lice had come from the refugee camp, but my uncle kept complaining to me that we had brought this trouble from home. He even claimed that Mother had not looked after us properly and had not kept us away from dirt and pests. It was very painful for me to have to listen to this. I felt insulted for Mother, who actually exaggerated when it came to cleanliness. She wouldn't let me grow the braids I wanted so badly, and we always had short haircuts so that she could look after us more easily.

In any event, for the next few evenings, our aunt put us through the same ritual. We each had our hair smeared and combed to get rid of the lice, but a long time passed before we were completely rid of them.

In the meantime, the war continued and daily air raids on Budapest took their toll. Most basic items were rationed, and it was very difficult to obtain food. The black market flourished and money was worth less and less. Aunt and

Uncle had a hard time providing for five children, so it was decided that Miriam, who was now seven, would go to live with Uncle Herman, a bachelor of about 30, who was a teacher and cantor. He lived in a small town about 60 kilometers from Budapest. Miriam was very attached to me—I was like a mother for her—and didn't want to go, but Uncle Jeno promised she would have a good time there.

"Poor Miriam!" Omer said, stopping me in the middle of the story. "And your aunt and uncle—how could they be so insensitive: to send a little girl to live with a bachelor, even if they were sorry about it and had no choice! What kind of life did they think she would have there, with him? And if they had to send one of you, why not you, the oldest?"

"I think they had a few reasons for that," I replied. "First, as a girl of 13, I could help out in the house and look after the little girls when my aunt and uncle were out. But Miriam was considered an extra burden on the family. Also, it was out of the question to send an adolescent girl to live alone with an unmarried man. I think that was the main reason for my aunt's decision. So my little sister was chosen, and she was very upset."

But within a week, Uncle Herman brought Miriam back. The girl was crying all the time, he said, and wouldn't do what she was told. He was having a hard time handling her. His housekeeper had helped, but even she soon gave up. Even though only a week had gone by, the little sister I saw had changed so much. Her black hair, which I used to take such pleasure in combing, was tied strangely with a ribbon on the top of her head. The clothes she wore were too big for her by at least two sizes and reached down to her ankles. She looked dazed, thin and pale.

As soon as she came in she ran to me, put her arms around my waist, and hugged me strongly, whispering, "I don't want to stay with Uncle Herman, I want to be with you." Seeing this, Aunt Mariska decided that Miriam would remain with us. Some wealthy relatives helped provide for us, so we were united again. Every day I combed her hair and looked after her, and we were together all the time.

In the middle of January 1944, we were enrolled in a school, even though nearly half the school year was already over. I was placed in fourth grade, which was two grades below my age level, and Miriam went to first grade instead of second grade. When I entered the classroom, the teacher introduced me as a refugee girl who had been adopted and asked the pupils to help make me feel at home. In the past I was always one of the shortest children in the class, but now, for the first time, I was the tallest because everyone else was two years younger. My Hungarian helped me mostly in conversation and in oral questions, but I quickly closed the gap in writing. In subjects such as arithmetic and drawing, where mastery of the language was not essential, I had no trouble.

At home I had enjoyed going to school, but here I went without enthusiasm and with the feeling that I had no choice. I felt bored and that it was all a big waste; socially, I didn't fit in either and didn't enjoy myself, probably because of the age difference. But Aunt and Uncle, who didn't know how long we would be staying with them or if we would ever go home again, wanted us to have a normal life like other children and not to feel like abandoned refugees.

As I said, the postal service was barely operating, even between neighboring countries, so hardly any letters arrived from Mother and Father. The ones that we did get were sadder and sadder, hinting that things were getting worse, despite what seemed to be a high probability that the end of the war was finally in sight. In this period, the Germans suffered heavy losses on all fronts and it was obvious that they were going to be defeated. After the famous long battle of Stalingrad, in Russia, the reports were that the Germans were retreating to the west, toward Slovakia, so I was naturally concerned for Mother and Father.

In March 1944, we learned that as the Russian front in the east, on the Ukrainian side, drew closer to Slovakia, the Slovak government intended to round up the few Jews who still remained in the eastern part of the country and exile them to camps in Poland, to ensure that they did not help the approaching Russians. However, in a brilliant ploy, and with the help of large bribes, the heads of the Jewish communities in western and northern Slovakia arranged for the Jews to be transferred to them. (A relatively large number of transports had been carried out in the east, such as in Michalovce, and many more Jews remained in the west.) The communities in the west lodged the Jews from the east in their houses or found them other shelter. In fact, most of the non-Jewish population in eastern Slovakia was also evacuated to the west of the country, because of the heavy fighting in the east. A few Jewish families succeeded in joining these evacuees, posing as non-Jews with the help of false papers, and survived.

Even before this movement began, Jews were being rounded up in the provincial towns of Hungary. At first, they were herded into ghettos, and then the inhabitants of several ghettos were moved into enormous brick factories, which also had huts for drying the bricks, and were able to house a large number of people. My sister Rachel was taken with our grandparents to a ghetto in the district town near their village. We learned that Mother and Father sent an "emissary" to our grandparents in the ghetto, who smuggled my sister out. Fortunately, they were not caught and she was taken back across the border by side roads and rejoined our parents.

Mother and Father were still in our hometown, preparing to leave for the west. Rachel found Mother in a serious psychological state: she said she was tired of living, because she didn't believe she would ever see her children again. Now, with one of the three, at least, having come back, she recovered her mental and physical health somewhat, although she would still become deeply depressed and declare that she wanted to put an end to her life.

In the meantime, Budapest was bombed intensively by the Allies and we spent many hours in shelters. Thousands of people were killed or wounded in the air raids, and tens of thousands were left homeless. The atmosphere became extremely difficult. In school, too, the air raid alarm often sounded and we went down into the shelter. Once, when we were on our way home, an air raid caught us on a crowded street. People began to run, hysterically looking for shelters in houses or in public places. We ran too, until we found a place where people took us in. We were trapped in the shelter for a few hours, and when we got out it was almost dark. Aunt Mariska was very worried about us, and the truth is that after this I was afraid to go to school.

Our relatives' apartment was on the second floor of a building located on one of the main streets of the Jewish section of Budapest. It would soon be inside the Jewish ghetto. Above us, on the third floor, there was another Jewish family, consisting of parents and a boy of 14. Every day, when we girls would play on the porch on the front side of the building, the boy from upstairs would go out to his porch and bombard me with questions: where did I come from, why did I leave my parents' house, how long would I be here, and so on. We became friends, and once in a while he came to visit us. After a time, he invited me to go with him to the magnificent Great Dohány Synagogue of Budapest, where he sang in a children's choir, mainly on Shabbat and holy days. He had a lovely high voice (which hadn't yet changed) and he was an excellent accordion player.

One Saturday, I agreed to go with him. I was charmed by the beauty and size of the synagogue, both outside and inside. I was thrilled by the service and listened with uplifted spirit to the singing of the choir, which was accompanied by an organ. It was, of course, the first time in my life I had ever seen anything like this. Before this, I could never even have imagined that an organ would be played in a synagogue. But my new friend explained to me that this was the custom in the Reform movement—it was also the first time I had ever heard of that current in Judaism.

The boy seemed very attracted to me. Almost every day he sent me love notes attached to a rope that he lowered from his porch to ours. The little girls—my sister and my cousins Györgyi and Vali—would snatch the notes and refuse to let me have them until I promised to read them aloud—they didn't know how to read yet. It was all very amusing. I was flattered at being courted. The relationship with him and the notes he sent provided some pleasant moments. The hours I spent with him made me forget the longings I felt for my parents and our house. I was proud that the neighbors' boy liked me. We read books together and went for walks in the streets of the city, and he told me about its history. We stayed in touch until I immigrated to Israel, and when he and his parents arrived here we renewed our friendship and he played the accordion in my honor at my wedding.

The Germans suffered one defeat after another on the Eastern Front, but that did not stop them from transporting and murdering Jews. In March 1944, around the same time we heard the rumors from Slovakia, there was a great commotion in our apartment building, most of whose tenants were Jews. The rumor spread like wildfire: the Germans had entered Budapest and were marching through the streets as though they were the victors and not the defeated. We hurried to the window to see the parade, which passed down our street, too, and we saw the Germans go by in jeeps and on motorcycles, and in armored vehicles that were packed with armed troops. Then infantry soldiers marched by in broad columns, projecting power and force, despite the rumors that their defeat was near at hand. The procession went on and on; it seemed endless.

When I saw this spectacular display, I knew for certain that the old tension and fear would return and that this was the end of the "safe" haven with our aunt and uncle. Another threatening period was beginning, and who could say where it would lead? What were the Germans planning to do in Hungary? Would they round up the Jews, as they did in Slovakia, and send them to the east, or would the Jews be protected by the Hungarian people, in whom they placed so much trust? The answers to these questions were not long in coming.

Third Escape, or the Return Home

A month later, in April 1944, I was still in Budapest. The Allies' planes were still bombing the city heavily day and night, without let-up. This was known as "carpet-bombing." The attacks were aimed at specific targets, but they covered a large area and also damaged places that were not specified as targets. Going down to the shelter became a routine part of life. The wail of the air-raid siren sent everyone scurrying beneath the ground, and the same siren announced the end of the air raid — at least until the next time.

When we came out of the shelter after an air raid, our surroundings looked different. High-rises had disappeared and furniture and other household objects protruded from the rubble like the exposed innards of a lost life. Other sirens now wailed — ambulances rushed the injured to the hospitals, while those who were less fortunate and had been in buildings that took a direct hit were removed lifeless from the rubble. The carcasses of animals, their organs shattered, lay all about. The very air seemed to be scorched, and a stench of death hung over everything.

Despite the danger and the fear of being hurt in the bombing raids, we kept wishing for them to continue and were happy when they did, hoping that they would hasten the Germans' surrender. Nevertheless, the Germans and their henchmen continued to impose new decrees on the Jews. Jews were forbidden to employ non-Jews, so my aunt's live-in housekeeper had to leave. Even though the Germans knew their end was near, they wanted to finish carrying out the vicious plan of extermination that they had begun in other countries in Europe. Now came the turn of Hungary's Jews.

The Jews in the provincial towns were herded into ghettos within a few weeks. Some tried to flee, mainly to Romania, or to reach Budapest, where it was easier to lose one's official identity and disappear into the crowd. Yet, even though portents abounded and refugees who arrived told about the atrocities in the death camps, only a few Jews tried to flee, though, in any case, flight was very difficult. Hardly anyone looked for an alternative—a hiding place. Young people, mainly those in Zionist youth movements, tried to get across the border. If they were caught, they were shot and their bodies were thrown into the Danube. Members of the "Arrow Cross"—named for the symbol of the Hungarian Nazis—also shot many of the adopted refugee children on the banks of the Danube, using the river to dispose of their bodies. The Danube ran red with Jewish blood. After all the Jews from the provinces had been deported to Auschwitz, the Germans decided to concentrate the Jews of Budapest in ghettos, ahead of their deportation.

Rumors about the rapidly worsening situation of the

Jews in Hungary reached the few Slovak Jews who were still alive, all of whom were now concentrated in a specified area in the north and west of Slovakia. My father, too, heard about the developments, and even though he was in a strange city and living on the charity of the local Jews, he was defiant and resourceful enough to send an emissary to fetch us away from the new inferno.

Thus it was that one fine day early in the morning, in the midst of these events, a dark-skinned man knocked on the door of our flat. He said he was a Gypsy who lived in Slovakia and also spoke Hungarian. His clothes were tattered, he was unshaven, and his appearance immediately made us all suspicious. But he showed us a letter from Father stating that he intended to reunite the family with the help of the bearer of the letter. Father had decided on this step because of the relative calm that prevailed then in Slovakia, which was reflected in the stability of the situation—meaning that there were no transports.

Our aunt and uncle weren't sure if they should do what Father asked and send us away with this dubious looking person. Wouldn't we be in great danger on such a long journey with all the fighting and bombing, and with the roads so unsafe? The man's sudden arrival, with no advance warning, made us very edgy. We had to make a quick decision. There was no time to lose, the man said, and there were preparations to make for the dangerous journey. Finally, what helped us decide was the feeling that it really would be preferable if we were with our parents, for better or for worse; and my cousin Simon, who was two years younger than me, would also go with us.

Right away, our aunt dressed us in several layers of clothing, so we wouldn't have to carry anything. We were given money and a few provisions for the way. Aunt and Uncle gave us their tearful blessing and accompanied us just as far as the gate, so as not to arouse attention. On the street, I looked up one last time and saw them standing in the window, blowing kisses. This parting evoked the same feeling of insecurity I had felt in similar situations in the past. I wanted to stay so much that my legs felt too heavy to lift. Seeing my hesitation, the man whispered a few words of encouragement in my ear—and I forced myself to start walking.

It was still early and the late-spring weather was pleasant. The streets were all but deserted, and the few people we saw hurried about their business, fearful of being caught on the street when the siren began to wail, as had lately happened several times a day. We saw quite a few German soldiers passing by on foot or in vehicles. I was very sad, gripped by a powerful feeling of distress that would not let go. As we got onto the train, it felt painfully familiar: Here we are sitting on the train, away from our Gypsy, and pretending that it is our right to be here—just as in the first attempt to flee, which failed.

This time, though, the difference was that we didn't have the feeling that we would be caught. Many people left the city to escape the bombings, which were directed mainly at the capital, Budapest. Most non-Jews who had relatives in rural areas went to stay there, or at least sent their children there. And because we too were supposedly getting away from the bombings, no one paid any attention to us. We made the long journey in a packed train and got off just before the border.

The man told us that we were going to make for the border immediately, and I asked why he didn't want to wait for night. But he reassured me, explaining that, because their situation was so serious, the Germans had sent all the available regular and reserve forces to the front and they did not have enough people to guard the borders. They didn't care any longer about anything, he said, and crossing the border was no problem. He was right. Where we were, the border ran through an open field, which we crossed without seeing anyone and without anyone bothering us.

The next train station we came to was in Slovakia, and once again I heard the language I knew. I was excited: Soon I would see Mother and Father again, after almost half a year. My little sister, who was now eight, and our cousin, stayed close by me. In the early afternoon, after a short trip, we reached the town of Nitra, in western Slovakia, where my parents had come after the Jews were removed from their homes in the eastern part of the country. Suddenly everything looked run-down and unimpressive after Budapest, which was divided into two by the broad Danube and had beautiful wide boulevards and magnificent tall buildings. Everything looked so tiny, like a drab provincial town. The buildings were taller than in our hometown, but everything looked very ordinary.

The man led us onto a side street and soon we came to a one-story house containing several apartments. We went through the gate into a square courtyard. The man knocked on the door of one of the flats. It opened slowly and hesitantly—and there was Father! He gave a great shout, stretched out his arms to embrace us, and called to Mother.

Father looked very shabby. He was unshaven and wore a strange kind of beret, and his trousers were held up sloppily by suspenders. This was not how I remembered him, and I felt a twinge of pity. We went in quickly and only then did I see Mother and my sister Rachel. I will never forget that moment. Mother was sitting on a chair, staring ahead vacantly as though she had no idea what was going on around her. I remembered her plump, always with a kerchief on her head, and now I saw an old woman—yet she was barely 44!—bare-headed, her hair uncombed, very thin, pale and wearing clothes that hung on her loosely.

Next to her was Rachel, whom I also barely recognized, even though it was only six months since I last saw her. She was much taller now, very thin, and wore a frightened look. Mother didn't even get up when we entered, as though she didn't know what was happening. Later I learned that because of her serious psychological condition, which was caused by worry about us, she took tranquilizers that clouded her senses.

I looked around at the room in which my parents and sister were living. It was a tiny space, barely nine square meters, and had no washroom. The furniture consisted of two beds, a small, shaky table, and two chairs. There were two boxes in one of the corners, containing the few clothes and other items that they brought from home. The room was quite crowded with all of us in it, and the sense of being cramped made me feel even more restless. Despair over-whelmed me at the pathetic sight of the hovel and my family, and I started sobbing loudly. I cried for my parents and I cried for myself and my fate, for having to leave a lovely, orderly home for this place of abject poverty. I wept for a long time, totally ignoring everyone around me.

Soon the man who had brought us received his payment and left. Little by little, I calmed down. We sat down to talk. Now Mother wept silently. Perhaps our arrival had jolted her into a greater awareness of the situation—at least that her girls were all back safe and sound. A few days later, I learned that during the whole time we were gone, Mother had never stopped blaming herself for agreeing to the separation, and had lost her will to live. When my sister Rachel came back, after being taken out of the ghetto where she had been sent with our grandparents, she never left Mother's side and even thwarted several suicide attempts— once, for example, Mother wanted to throw herself in front of a train. All these months, Rachel had been our mother's guardian angel when she was certain that Miriam and I were dead and did not want to go on living. She had become even more distraught after hearing that Arrow Cross troops were shooting adopted children on the banks of the Danube.

We were all supposed to live in this one small space. Because there was hardly room for even the five of us, Father sent our cousin Simon to a shelter run by the Jewish community for children and teenagers without parents. We stayed in Nitra from the end of May until September 7, 1944. Mother and Father worked a bit in their professions, or failing that, they looked for odd jobs and were barely able to provide for us. Almost every day we heard reports that the Germans were retreating on all fronts and that the day of salvation was at hand. In the meantime, we sometimes had to run for the shelters even here, though the air raids in this part of Slovakia were fewer and less intense. Every day, we awaited the miracle that would deliver us from our suffering, but in the meantime it did not occur.

For those few months, we did not go to school and the truth is that the whole period has been wiped completely out of my memory. I do know that partisans began to organize in the forests to fight the fascist regime, and they became stronger as their numbers grew. Some of the Jews who still remained also joined the guerrillas, who were supported by the Allies. Everyone hoped and wanted to believe that the war would soon end and that we would be spared. But then came that terrible day, September 7, and all our hopes were dashed. The new threat to our lives arrived like a sudden tempest, with no prior warning. And this time, nothing could help—not fictitious or genuine conversion, not money, not status, not an essential profession, not even connections with the right people. This time, no Jew would be more privileged than his fellow Jew: all were doomed to the same bitter fate....

The Last Transport

September 7, 1944. Morning. Father had gone to the synagogue, as he did every day. The moment he returned, I saw that he looked different. His hat was tilted to one side; he looked nervous and uneasy. He whispered something to Mother and her reaction showed that it was bad news. Unsteadily, Father went to the kitchenette and poured himself a cup of coffee from the pot Mother had prepared for him. He washed his hands and cut a slice of bread. Then he sat down on one of the rickety chairs, made the blessing over the bread and bit off a piece, and sipped his coffee loudly, all the while looking up and away, as though not daring to meet Mother's gaze.

Mother stared at him in astonishment for a bit before lashing out, "We are going to die and you sit there drinking coffee, as though nothing has happened?!"

Father said nothing and went on drinking his coffee. I shivered at his composure. I asked him why all the secrecy. Even though I was only 14, my parents considered me a responsible grown-up, and I had certainly proved that I could be trusted. Father would say only that he had heard in the synagogue that the Germans, though being routed on all fronts, had no intention of calling off the "Final Solution"—by which they meant disposing of all the Jews in occupied Europe—and in our case they would do it by means of Slovak informers. They were going to deport every last Jew to the camps, and fast. The order had already been given for all the Jews to pack their things, organize themselves, and report that very day for the transport. That would be the end of the small community, which had so far survived the twists and turns of fate. The remaining Jews in Slovakia would be sent to camps in the East, like most of the Jews in Europe. Much later, I learned that the pressure on the Jews was resumed because of the partisan uprising that followed the German invasion of Slovakia on August 29, 1944.

Father, with his resourcefulness and his naive faith, again refused to surrender. He would not go to the slaughter; it was his duty to defend and protect his family. Even though the situation was bleak and escape looked hopeless, even though nearly three years of flight and hiding had exhausted everyone, Father began to devise a new plan. His main problem was that we had no money at all and no place to turn. But, like a trapped animal that senses the oncoming danger, Father declared: "Come, we will go to the woodshed at the edge of the courtyard. That way, they won't find us here. We'll wait there for a few hours and then we'll see what to do next. Girls, you will have to stay absolutely quiet so we won't be discovered and so we can hear what's going on outside."

Mother, always practical and skeptical, had doubts. There was no escape this time, she said, and she would not go with Father. What was the point of waiting in the dark, moldy woodshed — in any case, we would be found when they searched the houses. And if by some miracle we weren't discovered, what would happen at night? Where would we go? Mother and Father were also anxious about the fate of our cousin Simon, who was with the other refugees under the community's protection. Would he be deported, or would he try to escape, despite his young age? It was only after the war that we learned, to our immense relief, that he had succeeded in getting away with the help of an older boy and had crossed the border back into Hungary and made it home safely.

Father finally managed to persuade Mother that his plan was at least worth a try. We quickly put on coats and stuffed some warm clothes and food into a bag. Little Miriam held on for dear life to her new rubber doll, as though it gave her security. Carrying these items, we rushed to the woodshed. Father quickly opened the lock, told us to enter, and closed the door. We sat down on a wide log. It was almost totally dark. There was no window, and only the cracks between the logs of the walls let in a bit of air.

Soon we heard the sound of people running and shouting in the courtyard. Through the cracks, we saw our neighbors rushing about to and fro, without any direction or purpose, like mice in a maze. Everyone was carrying knapsacks and arguing and consulting about what items to take. Then the police from the Hlinka Guard appeared and began pushing and shoving the people toward the assembly place. In an instant, the courtyard emptied out, a strange silence descended and a lone policeman went from one apartment to the next, placing a wax seal on each lock, as they did everywhere when a family was taken from its home.

Feeling numb, we sat huddled close to one another on the log. Father began to build a wall of logs between us and the door, to hide us in case someone suddenly opened the woodshed. We held hands, whispered a bit to one another, and only got up when we had to relieve ourselves, which we did in the far corner of the shed.

Hours passed. The sun began to go down. Angular rays pierced the cracks in the wall and illuminated the small room. Not a sound could be heard. We knew that all the Jews in our courtyard had been taken or had fled. There was only one non-Jewish family in the "Jews' courtyard," and we wondered how they must feel now that they had been left by themselves in the large, square courtyard, which had been emptied of all its other inhabitants. Their apartment was situated directly opposite the woodshed, and we could see how they looked out the window and once in a while opened the door, stepped outside for a second, and immediately went back in. The spectacle of the Jews being rounded up appeared to have left them embarrassed and bewildered. They had not tried to protest, or to offer any words of encouragement to the deportees. In fact, they had not even bothered to say farewell. They had stayed inside, because they were ashamed, frightened, or indifferent.

It was obvious that we could not remain in the woodshed without sufficient food and without anyone to turn to for help, and we knew that the place would almost certainly be searched. So, at Father's instructions, even before it was dark, we ventured out and walked across the way to the home of our gentile neighbors, and knocked on the door. They were stunned to see us, not understanding how we could still be there, and looked at us with both pity and fear. Father asked if we could stay with them for a bit, no longer than one night, but they absolutely refused and slammed the door in our faces.

We started to walk quickly, then to run, in the direction of the large forest that bordered the town. The streets were almost empty. The few people we passed must have realized that we were Jews on the run, but fortunately no one stopped us. They all went about their business, or pretended not to see us. Suddenly a young man in a policeman's uniform appeared out of nowhere, riding a bicycle. He stopped and got off in front of us. Our hearts skipped a beat: All was lost! Then suddenly, to our complete amazement, the young man smiled at us and said, "Children, run, run, escape, don't be afraid!" Then he mounted his bike and rode off. His words seemed to infuse us with renewed willpower and we ran even faster. I still remember exactly his heartening and uplifting words, and I believe the episode was a sign from heaven, to strengthen us.

Reaching the edge of the town, we found ourselves facing a broad cornfield. The kernels of corn were painted a rich gold color by the low rays of the setting sun, and the sheaves rustled in the soft wind. Observing this pastoral scene, I reflected that our flight was totally out of place and maybe even unreal, certainly absurd: everything was quiet and tranquil, and only we were agitated and in a rush, hurtling ourselves between the rows of green stalks. The corn grew thick and tall, and so hid us very well. The cobs were covered with juicy, ripe kernels, and in another day or two the harvest would begin. We ran our hands over the plants and then picked and ate some, even though they were neither peeled nor cooked. They were very tasty, though, and we ate our fill. Father urged us deeper into the field; here we would wait for nightfall and then we would cross the open area and enter the forest.

Suddenly we heard faint shouts, which became louder as they drew closer. Peeking out from between the stalks, we saw policemen approaching on the run.

"All Jews who are hiding in the corn are to come out immediately!" came a loud shout, followed by silence. No one obeyed. Suddenly a round of shots was fired into the dense growth. We froze. Then we heard a rustling noise close by, the trampling of feet crushing the plants, and frightened whispering. Dim figures emerged on our right and left, parting the corn as they moved toward the edge of the field. There were whispered arguments and attempts at persuasion. Some apparently thought it would be better to give themselves up to the police and hope they would not be killed, even if that meant being transported to a work camp, rather than face a certain death here from the riflemen....

We too were about to come out of our hiding place, for fear of being shot, but then Father shook his head firmly and signaled us to keep quiet and stand still. Peering through the stalks of corn, we saw a few Jews standing perfectly still, like us, waiting for events to take their course. For a moment, all was still. The air was fraught with despair. Those who were caught in the trap looked lost. There was a painful contrast between the beauty of nature and the brutal persecution.

Suddenly the silence was shattered by more shouted warnings and another ear-splitting round of firing into the field, which drove more people out of hiding. After a time, those who had surrendered started to walk back to the city, guarded by the captors. I remember shutting my eyes as tightly as I could so I would not have to watch. I was positive that everyone who came out of that cornfield would be shot on the spot. I felt a huge sense of relief after they all left. We continued to crouch down, silent and shaking—partly from fear and partly from the chill in the air. Miriam was crying but Father put his hand over her mouth so she wouldn't give us away. When the voices faded into the distance and silence reigned again, Father said that we had to make for the forest at once, before nightfall, otherwise we would not be able to see the path in front of us.

More than half a century has passed since that fateful autumn day on which we miraculously escaped, and I am still unable to fathom what happened. How did Father dare to lead us into that terribly dangerous adventure? Was he a hero, a prophet, or was he so childishly naive that he did not consider the possible consequences of his actions, the risks, the total impossibility that we would succeed? I can only imagine that, as he led us toward the forest, he possessed the senses of a hunted animal fleeing for its life. After all, our flight had no defined direction and most of the time we didn't know where we were, as the area was foreign to us. We had hardly any of the necessities for survival, and yet this man led his wife and his three daughters into "nowhere," into an endless sea of trees. What was his plan? Probably he had no plan at all, but just kept walking as though in a trance. Did he know where we would lay down our heads that night in the forest, what dangers lurked there, and how we would go on? Did he give a thought to what we would eat and how we would protect ourselves against the cold, which was already becoming sharp as autumn began? But like Father, who assumed the burden and the responsibility, we too ran like wild animals being pursued by a predator, smelling the danger and searching for shelter. Father was bold enough to uproot his family and send us charging into the unknown, with only one goal: to stay alive.

Finally, we reached the beginning of the forest. From afar we saw the outlying houses of the town. By now it was almost completely dark. The trees were dark and frightening, and the ground was covered with a layer of fallen leaves. After a while, before it grew totally dark, we reached a broad, flat clearing protected by large boulders at both ends. Father began to pick up broken branches and we helped by throwing away small stones. When we were done, we had a nearly smooth space where we could lie down and stretch out. Father told us to lie close to one another, for warmth, and said that the carpet of leaves would serve us as both a bed and a cover. Rachel, Miriam, and I lay down on the ground and covered ourselves with our coats, while Mother and Father piled leaves on us. The leaves really did keep out the cold. Before closing my eyes, I looked up to watch the branches swaying in the breeze and followed the leaves as they fluttered down, caught on the wind, before floating gently to the earth.

Utterly exhausted by the day's events, we fell into a deep sleep almost immediately. Amazingly, the leaves kept us as warm as any blanket, and I slept the whole night through without waking up even once. It's been more than 50 years since then, and whenever I see autumn leaves, I conjure up that scene in the forest—Father piling up the leaves and making a space for us to spend the night, and then covering us with them. I don't know whether Mother and Father also slept on that first night in the forest. I never asked them. The next day, after I awoke to the sound of birds chirping, the silence was broken only by the noises of the forest. The rays of the sun struggled to pierce the thick treetops. From now on, I felt, our lives would be different—we would be like wild animals fleeing from hunters.

From this point on, my story will be only partially accurate. Many of the things that happened and that we told ourselves may have taken on a different form—because, even though we experienced them then, when we looked back we could hardly believe it ourselves. In some cases, the events came back to me in the form of dreams and so their memory was preserved. But perhaps their image in my dreams was softer and more tolerable than the harsh reality. And certainly some things have been forgotten, as memories that evoke fear and anxiety are best left buried in the unconscious. Maybe that's a blessing....

Like Hansel and Gretel

"Grandmother, how could you really have stayed in the forest?" Omer asked when she came for her regular visit and wanted to hear what happened next. "What did you eat and how did you find your way? It must have been very scary to be outside at night and to wander around in a strange forest, without a place to go. Did any animals bother you?"

"So you want to know how we got along in the forest and how long we were there? I'm sorry, Omer, but I can't tell you. It's as though that whole time in the forest was all a dream and some parts are missing, even if others are whole and clear. Today I can hardly even imagine what it felt like to be afraid in that dark and threatening forest. When we talked about it later, we calculated that we must have been there between ten days and two weeks. None of us remembers exactly, because all the days were exactly the same, the surroundings didn't change and time seemed to stop. But there are a few scenes that are still vivid in my memory and take me back to that time. We were very lucky that it didn't rain in those early days of September and that the cold didn't yet freeze the ground on which we made our 'beds.' But now I will give you at least part of the answer to your question...."

The forest was huge and seemed to have no end. We made our way between the tall trees and every once in a while we came to a clearing that broke the continuity of the woods. The local farmers used these areas to grow different crops and seasonal vegetables. We scoured the clearings for vegetables or anything else that the farmers had missed. We always found a few tomatoes, a head of cabbage, some juicy cucumbers, or at least wild strawberries, which were our main food. It's as though they had been left deliberately, so that we would collect them, like the gleanings in the Bible. Our aim in the forest was to get as far as we could from Nitra, from where Jews were being transported, and make for one of the nearby villages. We walked slowly, venturing into those clearings every once in a while to restore our souls, then rushing back to the shelter of the trees. Sometimes we came across thin trickles of water falling from the heights, and we could quench our thirst.

Making our way through the dense forest, we looked for spaces where the sun penetrated, creating trails of light and warmth. It was there that we rested. We listened to the chirping of the birds, we watched their flight with great interest, and we concluded that they were getting ready for their winter journey. At dusk, great flocks swooped into the treetops and prepared for the night, all the while sounding their bird lullabies in a delightful chorus. Lying on the ground, we watched them as though we were spectators at a play, almost forgetting why we were there. Sometimes I witnessed fierce battles between them, such as when one bird found a seed and another would attack it and try to snatch the morsel from its beak. If the first bird fought back, a struggle took place, with the seed constantly passing back and forth from one bird to the other. I would keep my fingers crossed for the bird that originally found the food, hoping it would eat the seed before the assailant stole it. Sometimes both of them lost to a third bird, and then the first two combatants would look at each other as though to say, "What a pity we fought, now we've both lost."

Occasionally, we saw squirrels dart between the trees. When we stayed in one spot for a time, perhaps to rest, the squirrels gradually got used to our presence and became brave enough to approach us. Exotic insects and brilliantly colored butterflies flitted among the trees. Night creatures —crawlers and rodents—would sometimes appear and scare us almost to death. The day was filled with sounds of all kinds, but at night, when it was pitch black and the birds stopped chirping and only the wind whistled between the branches of the trees and murmured in our ears, we were seized by an uncontrollable fear that someone would suddenly leap out of the dark and attack us. I don't know which was more frightening—the animals of the forest or the thought of a *gardist* who would take us by surprise.

One day, as we walked along in a column—as we always did, with Father leading and Mother at the rear, we heard the sound of voices approaching. By the time we tried to figure out what to do, it was too late to turn in another direction and get away. We were about to be discovered. All we could do was hastily decide that, if asked, we would say that we were hiking for pleasure and collecting berries (which we did in fact find from time to time).

Three young people appeared from between the trees:

two men and a woman, who all looked to be in their early twenties. Then we recognized the young woman—she was the daughter of one of the Jewish families in the town. We all breathed a huge sigh of relief. They smiled at us, edgily at first, but then they quickly relaxed and were no longer afraid. They said they were surprised to find a family with children here and told us how brave we were to hide in the forest in our situation.

They had disguised themselves as gentiles and obtained false papers, they said, and sometimes did odd jobs for farmers. But when suspicions arose about their identity, they had left immediately, before it was too late, and were now trying to reach the partisans in the mountains. They knew they faced a long and dangerous journey. Naturally, they absolutely rejected the idea, which Father raised, that we join them—as the guerrilla fighters lived in harsh field conditions and could not accept families with children.

We parted tearfully, wishing one another good luck and success. When the three young people had disappeared into the depths of the forest, and the stillness seemed to become even more intense, I again felt alone and trapped. How could we keep hiding in the forest without the food and other items we needed to maintain ourselves? We seemed to be walking in circles, aimlessly retracing our steps, encountering the same trees and bushes and even the same clearings—but without seeing any light at the end of the tunnel. But Father, who calculated our route according to the position of the sun when it rose and set, was certain that we were headed toward the villages. And even if we had doubts about his navigation, we had no other choice under the circumstances.

So we kept on "advancing" toward our "nowhere." One day we spied another large clearing, where the ground was covered with greenish-yellow grass. Through the trees, we seemed to see figures moving about. When we got closer, we saw a brown cow standing idly and chewing its cud and next to the cow a peasant woman wearing a broad, dark skirt and a black kerchief that was tied in a knot beneath her chin. She held a long stick in one hand and rested her other hand on a tall pail of milk. She seemed to be waiting for the cow to finish eating.

Mother immediately decided on her own to come out of hiding and ask the woman for some milk. She approached the woman as we watched with bated breath.

Seeing Mother suddenly step into the clearing, the peasant woman exclaimed in a frightened voice, "Jesus and Mary, who are you and where did you come from?"

Mother replied in Hungarian, hoping that she would understand, as she knew that few people spoke Hungarian in this region of Slovakia: "Please, help me, give me a little milk for my children and God will reward you."

The woman drew back, clearly agitated. She looked around in confusion, but apparently could not refuse Mother's pleading eyes and poured about two cups of milk into a bowl. But she also kept repeating a few words in broken Hungarian: "*Fele, fele melonek*" (meaning, "I scared they shoot to me").

Obviously stunned by this completely unexpected meeting, the woman shook her head back and forth, as though to say she couldn't believe her eyes, and remained rooted to the spot even after Mother disappeared from her sight back into the trees where we were waiting. After a while we saw her shooing the cow rapidly in the opposite direction, as though a demon was chasing her.

The fresh milk was a real treat. As little girls, we were very spoiled and often refused to eat, and we especially didn't like milk. But all that now seemed to be a dream. We were very hungry, the aroma of the milk made our mouths water, and the three of us swiftly and avidly finished off the unexpected delicacy. The sentence the peasant woman repeated in her broken Hungarian has stayed with us all these years, and we still make use of it. Whenever we find ourselves in a frightening situation, one of us will almost always chant "*Fele, fele melonek,*" and the others immediately understand....

The next day, when there seemed to be no more possibilities of finding food, we finally saw the houses of a village through the trees. Hope of obtaining food drove us on. It was hard to estimate the distance to the village, and we started arguing about it. But not only about that. What do we do now? How could we know what the best time would be to leave the forest, enter the village, and try to buy food? And who would carry out the mission? Mother and Father agonized, and finally Father pointed at me and said, "You are already a grown-up girl. I will give you money and show you the best way to get to the village. When you get there, look for a general store" — there was one in every farming settlement, no matter how small — "and buy as much food as you can with the money."

Mother objected vigorously: "The wandering in the forest has made you lose your mind! How do you even dare to think of sending the girl into the village alone, to a completely strange place? You are sending her straight to the depths. I say no!"

Naturally, Father would have gone himself, but his appearance would have given him away at once; and Mother, of course, was not fluent in the local language—so I was the logical choice.

By the time Mother and Father settled their quarrel, it was too late to carry out the plan. But the next morning, when we were on the verge of real hunger, the decision was made. I tried to reassure Mother, telling her that I would easily be able to do it and to get food for all of us.

Poor Mother, she was always afraid. Even in less dangerous situations, she would protect us with all her might. And what a difficult test fate had in store for her this time! She had to agree to a risky adventure in which her young daughter would disappear from her sight and supervision and perhaps be caught, never to return! However, seeing no other option, she gave in to our pleas, but with a heavy heart.

I walked toward the edge of the forest with the money Father had given me in my coat pocket. As in the story of Hansel and Gretel, who made sure they knew how to get back to their home by leaving bread crumbs on the path, I decided to memorize the location of trees and stones that I passed on the way, so I could find my way back. At the edge of the forest I saw a wide field in front of me. I had to make sure I would be able to find the place to enter the forest when I returned. Turning around, I looked at the dense, dark forest, in which all the trees looked alike, trying to find something unusual that would be easy to identify. Then I noticed one tree that stood out from the others: Its branches had a tremendous spread and the trunk was so thick that even three people would probably not be able to put their arms around it. With a sharp stone I cut into the dark brown bark and made a round white mark, hoping I would spot the huge tree with the bald spot on its trunk when I got back from the village. I also built a small pile of stones in front of the tree. As I walked, I dropped pine cones and prayed that I would be able to find the path again. The whole time, I was thinking about what a good thing it was that there were wise children's tales, and how lucky I was to remember them and be able to make use of one of their ideas.

I started walking faster, and as I left the forest behind me, I felt terribly lonely and more and more worried that I would not succeed in my mission. For a moment, I even thought of turning around and going back, but the great responsibility that had been given to me and the lack of any other alternative strengthened me, and I walked on. Reaching the village, I entered an unpaved street with small, low houses on both sides, most of them with thatched roofs, though in some cases the roofs were tiled, and with fences around the yards. A woman in one of the yards looked at me curiously, and when I asked her where the general store was I had the feeling that she had guessed my identity. But she looked indifferent and only pointed toward the store, which was very close by.

I hesitated before entering the square, wooden store — again I wanted to turn and run away as fast as I could. But I overcame my fears, walked up the three shaky wooden stairs that led to a low door and went in. The store was small and dark, and smelled strongly of smoke and spices. When my eyes adjusted to the dimness, I saw a tall, middle-aged man, wearing a cap, standing behind the counter. Next to him another man sat on a high stool. Both of them looked at me curiously. On the walls were half-empty shelves: There was very little merchandise. I tried to figure out what to buy, since there was very little to choose from. Would they even sell me anything in the middle of a war? Most goods were supplied only in return for ration coupons that the authorities distributed, and of course I had no coupons.

The shopkeeper gave me an encouraging smile and asked what I wanted. "Food!" I wanted to say, but I knew I had to ask for particular items, so I said, "Could I have some bread, and also butter and margarine?"

He went over to one of the shelves and picked up a pretty big loaf of bread—dark, round country bread. Without my asking, he placed other items on the counter, besides margarine. There was a slice of high-fat cheese on a dish, a sausage with a coarse whitish peel, and a jar of jam. The man gave me a wink and said, "You will probably be wanting all these things, if you are strong enough to carry them." It was obvious that he had guessed my identity and understood that I was going to take the food to others who were waiting somewhere. His eyes seemed kind, and I somehow knew that he wished me no ill—on the contrary, he wanted to help. Picking up the sausage, I asked him what it was made of. "Oh, that's an excellent sausage," he replied cordially, "it's made out of horsemeat."

I put down the sausage at once. I knew that horsemeat was not kosher and would never be found on our table. Father, who kept strictly kosher, would refuse to touch it, despite our situation, and he might even stop his daughters from eating it. I wondered whether the nice man would be insulted if I rejected his generosity, so in the end I took the sausage, too, despite my hesitations. The price the man asked for the goods seemed very low. There was enough money left for a few sweets that I added to the purchase. I said goodbye and left carrying two well-wrapped but heavy parcels.

As I walked back, I felt eyes watching me from behind drawn curtains and through the cracks in the fences around the yards. Or maybe I only imagined it, and my excitement made me blow everything up out of all proportion. But my heart swelled with happiness, as I had successfully carried out the mission. I tried to walk nonchalantly, as though I was not in a hurry, but as soon as I left the main street and reached the edge of the village I started to walk faster. Then I was almost running across the wide field, toward the forest that loomed in front of me. The parcels were heavy, but the satisfaction I felt at getting the food filled me with pride and the burden hardly seemed to slow me down. It was enough food for two or three days and maybe more.

I reached a tree with sweeping branches and I was certain that this was where I had left the forest. Here I would enter between the trees and follow the trail that would take me back to my family. I looked for the first signs—the pile of stones and the white spot on the tree trunk—but I couldn't find them. I felt a sharp twinge of fear: What if I couldn't find my way back? What if this was the wrong place?! I came out of the forest again and started looking around, walking slowly and looking very carefully to try to find the signs.

Finally I saw the pile of stones on my right, I found the tree with the peeled bark, and with a tremendous feeling of relief I retraced my steps. All the signs I had left greeted me, but as I entered more deeply into the forest, I thought that by this time I should have reached my parents and sisters. The way seemed endless, much longer than it was before. The parcels weighed me down, and every few steps I was seized anew by the fear that I was lost and would never find my way out again. I suddenly remembered long-forgotten frightening stories about people who were lost in the forest and were never heard of again. My mouth went dry, I almost choked with fear, but I went on.

A few minutes later I heard voices and the sounds of someone crying, which grew louder as I approached. What a feeling of joy and relief when I recognized the voices of my family! With a burst of energy I started to run, the branches whipping against me. I even stumbled and fell a few times. But when I reached them I saw a terrible sight: Father was standing passively in front of Mother, who was screaming and crying, pummeling him with her fists and shouting, "You sent our daughter to her death! God, why did I agree? Let's all go and give ourselves up to a transport, because that is the only place we will find the girl."

Then they saw me and fell silent. Mother lowered her arms listlessly. Father ran to me with tearful eyes, took the parcels and hugged me to him, whispering, "My darling,

God has again instructed you to help us and you succeeded again! This is another good sign, and we will certainly come out of the inferno safely."

Mother continued to sob silently, though now her tears were of joy and relief. She too embraced me and then sat down on the ground, totally drained. Father examined the parcels. When he came to the sausage, he didn't ask, but I said apologetically, "It is made of horsemeat, Father, because the war is on and it's hard to find cows."

Father said nothing, but he did not touch the sausage. We girls and Mother ate the non-kosher food heartily. Thanks to the food, we were able to hide out in the forest for a few more days and to continue toward a distant village that Father had heard about.

Farewell to Life in the Forest

The food I bought in the village ran out within three or four days, even though we ate very sparingly. The days grew shorter and the nights became cold. The time had come to end our stay in the forest. After coming to the edge of the forest, we decided to leave its shelter and make for one of the villages in the vicinity, in the hope that we would be able to find a place to hide there—and, with luck, perhaps encounter a kind-hearted farmer. Only if we found someone humane, who would agree to hide us and not hand us over to the authorities, would we have a chance to survive. We knew very well that anyone who hid us faced a stiff punishment, that he would be risking his own life and his family's safety. Few people gave Jews shelter; the majority collaborated willingly with the Nazis and informed on Jews. So our decision to leave the forest was not an easy one. But we had no choice. In leaving, we knew that our fate hung in the balance. The forest had given us a certain security and had protected us as long as we stayed there.

We gathered our few belongings and entered the open area that stretched to the horizon. We started to walk. If anyone had seen us emerging from the trees, looking warily in all directions like hunted animals, he would surely have rubbed his eyes in disbelief and asked where these strange, shabby figures had suddenly come from and what they were doing far from any human habitation.

The sun was already beginning to go down. We walked along a paved road and left the forest ever farther behind. After proceeding some distance, we reached a large junction. Which road to take? We had four directions to choose from, but we hadn't the slightest idea where any of the roads led. Should we decide by "eenie-meenie-minie-moe"? Then Father remembered that the three young people we had met in the forest a week earlier said they were headed north, in the hope of reaching a city called Banska Bystrica. The uprising of the partisans there had drawn the whole region into their ranks. The local residents, sick and tired of the occupation, had joined the rebels. Their success in liberating occupied areas from the Germans and their henchmen, and their declaration of those areas as free, attracted thousands of young people and enabled many who had been hiding in the underground to escape to freedom. Jews, too, emerged from their hiding places. Everyone hoped that the fighters would expand their activity and liberate their occupied country region by region.

"We will go there too," Father stated, "and we too will have a chance to live in freedom and security."

Navigating by the sun, Father set off briskly and we followed.

Suddenly, I felt a weight in my chest and my heart started to pound. My hands and legs grew heavy. I collapsed onto a boulder at the junction. I started to choke. I couldn't understand what was happening to me. Mother and Father asked me what was wrong—I must have turned pale, too—and whether I felt ill. I broke into tears. I was inconsolable. I myself didn't know why I was crying, and all I could do was whisper, "I don't want to go to the partisans. Let's not go there, Father. Let's go this way"—and I pointed in the opposite direction.

My parents were astonished and couldn't fathom my strange request. They tried to persuade me to take the direction Father had decided on, but I continued to insist and to repeat over and over, "No, we mustn't go there!"

I didn't know then, and I still don't know, what got into me and why I was so insistent. When Mother and Father saw that they couldn't change my mind and that I was hanging on to the boulder for dear life and refusing to budge, they fell silent and looked at each other. I saw their eyes meet and I knew that they were going to agree with me and consider the event the hand of fate. Exhausted physically and mentally, I couldn't understand my stubbornness or explain my bizarre behavior.

In 1945, after the liberation, we learned that the uprising at Banska Bystrica was put down on October 27, 1944. Some of the resistance fighters fled into the hills in central Slovakia, but the rest were caught, tortured, and executed. Nearly all the Jews who had come out of hiding and gone there to join the resistance fighters were brutally executed. Hardly any of them managed to flee with the partisans. One of the survivors, a cousin of my good friend Yehudit—a boy of my age whom I met after the war—told me that his whole family, including my childhood friend Yehudit, had been executed before his eyes. He had managed to hide and watched through a crack in the wall as, to his mounting horror, they were tortured and murdered.

We set out again in the new direction. Soon, as the sun was setting, we saw a village on the horizon — small houses with pine trees scattered between them.

"We will try our luck here," Father declared.

We had no information or any clue to guide us in choosing which door to knock on. By the time we drew close to the first house in the village, it was already completely dark and only the lights shining through the windows guided our way. The house was isolated, located at a distance from the village proper. It was small and modest. It was also different from the other houses because it was exposed, without trees or greenery of any kind around it. As we approached, dogs in the more distant yards started to bark loudly. "Hurry," Father urged us, "let's knock here before the whole village comes out to see why the dogs are barking."

Father knocked a few times, until finally the door opened. In the faint light of the entrance we saw a young, sloppily dressed peasant. He stared at us curiously, surveyed us from top to bottom, and asked what we wanted. Father asked if we could come in and the man agreed. Father told him that we needed a place to hide until the troubles ended. Could he help us and let us stay? Naturally, we would pay for this service.

It was a one-room house with barely any furnishings. The peasant's young wife was looking after an infant who was asleep in a cradle that stood in one corner of the room. In the opposite corner, there was a very wide bed piled high with quilts of down, as was the custom in peasant homes. There was also a wooden crate that probably contained the family's belongings. Attached to the room was a tiny space where there were two wide gas burners and a pipe that ran to the ceiling and was connected to the chimney, which removed the smoke from the stove. A few cooking utensils hung on the wall above the burners. Despite the room's meagerness, it had a pleasant warmth, which made us feel relaxed and at home — a feeling we had almost forgotten. A fire burned in the stove. Its flickering flames cast colorful dancing shadows on the walls and helped to illuminate the dark room, in which a lone kerosene lamp gave off a bit of light. The walls were bare, apart from a large crucifix on one of them.

The man immediately agreed to let us stay. Although there was only the one bed, that would not be a problem, he said, as he and his family could sleep in the produce shed in the courtyard on a bed of straw and we could sleep in their bed.

We couldn't believe our ears. Stunned by his instant agreement, we felt a tremendous sense of relief and were deeply grateful. For a moment we wondered if it wasn't a trap of some kind, because the luck that had brought us to precisely this house seemed impossible. But we found that he was trying to help us honestly and sincerely. He and his wife gave us a little food, which we of course accepted willingly and immediately devoured. Father offered Jozef, for that was the peasant's name, money for our lodging. In our terms it was not enough for what he was doing for us. However, our money was running out quickly and Father intended to use it mainly to buy food.

Jozef's eyes lit up when he heard what Father was offering and immediately agreed, even saying he would give us as much food as he could get hold of. He was also ready to hide us for more than one night, in the hope that the war would end soon "and you will be able to go back to your home," he said kindly.

He and his wife went to the shed, which was also a barn for their one cow, to prepare their lodgings for the night. Left alone, we looked at one another in disbelief at our good fortune in finding this couple and at not having to spend the night under the stars. Then, exhausted by the events of the day, we lay down on the wide bed and gave thanks to God for guiding us on our way and leading us to this haven.

We stayed with the compassionate peasant for a week or ten days. His wife offered to launder our clothes. She made us tasty rabbit soup—they raised rabbits in cages—though Father still refused to touch non-kosher food and made do with bread, dairy products and vegetables. It rained heavily during the week and we counted our blessings in having a roof above our heads and not being in the forest. No one visited our hosts while we were there; maybe the bad weather and the autumn chill kept people indoors after they finished harvesting the summer crops. There is one thing that I do remember: We helped shell peas and shuck corn, but I don't remember how we washed, for example, or how we spent most of the day. Every evening Father paid the amount that had been agreed on, and everything seemed promising and tranquil.

One day, though, Jozef burst into the room in great agitation. He had bad news: We had to leave that very day because German troops had arrived in the village (which was called Cabaj-Čapor). They had fled from the front, which was close to Slovakia, and intended to stay in the village. They would certainly look around for places to sleep and we would all be in great danger if they found us.

With a heavy heart we decided to leave the house that had opened its door to us, as its occupants had opened their hearts. Jozef said he would accompany us part of the way and show us how to get to a neighboring village called Jarok, where we would be able to get help, he said. When night fell, we tearfully parted from his wife. She gave us a bit of food for the way and also the small bundle of clothes she had washed for us. We left the house feeling very downcast.

Accompanied by Jozef, we started to walk toward an uncultivated field. We were all highly emotional. My sisters cried and begged Mother and Father to stay in the house we had become so attached to in the short time we had been there. From a distance, we saw a few electricity poles, which marked the road to which Jozef was leading us. He burst into tears as we parted and wished us luck, saying he hoped we would meet again.

So once more we took the "wanderer's staff" and set out on an unknown road to an unknown destination. Mother whispered to Father—but I heard what she said—that perhaps it was time we turned ourselves in and joined one of the transports, to end the nightmare of wandering with its constant fears, insecurity, and uncertainty about what tomorrow would bring. How long could we go on like this? In the end they will catch us anyway, Mother said. But Father did not relent; stubbornly and persistently, he pressed on. We followed, almost asleep on our feet, late into the night, our path lit by the moon and the electricity poles that stretched to the horizon.

At about midnight, we saw from a distance wooden structures scattered about an open space. Coming closer, we found ourselves in the middle of a field that had already been harvested. We entered one of the structures and discovered that it was a sort of silo containing an enormous pile of grain and straw, which filled the interior almost completely. The straw served both as a bed and to cover us. We crawled deep inside. The pungent aroma inside the straw pile has always remained with me—any chance encounter with that aroma immediately takes me back to that silo in the remote Slovakian village of Jarok. The sharp ends of the straw pricked us, but the "mattress" was soft, and best of all, we could plow deep into it, so we were protected from the bitter cold. We fell asleep at once.

When we got up the next morning, we saw Father standing at the entrance to the silo and surveying the area. The sun sent warm rays into the structure. As we crawled out of the straw, we began to laugh—bits and pieces of straw stuck out of our hair and made us look like clowns. We helped one another pluck out the straw and we counted to see who had collected the most pieces... It was an ideal place to hide, except for the problem of food. We had already eaten the little bit that Jozef's wife had given us and were left with nothing. What were we going to do? Which of us would go to look for food? Where? How?

Then a decision was made that, to this day, I find hard to believe and incredibly daring. Nevertheless, it was carried out exactly as planned. Mother and Father decided that the two little ones would go to the village and ask for food. They thought that Rachel and Miriam would have a better chance of arousing the pity of simple, kind village folk.

I have never understood how my parents found the nerve to send my younger sisters on such a dangerous mission, or how they agreed to go. Didn't they worry about the dogs, and about the dogs' owners? But the rumbling of our stomachs and the survival instinct made us come up with ploys and ideas that were improbably bold—and more than a little dangerous.

The Tokoly Family

We had been in the silo for an entire day when Rachel and Miriam set out for the village to look for food. My parents and I waited with bated breath for them to return. Mother and Father were afraid that they had abandoned the little ones to their fate by sending them on a mission that was well beyond their age. We watched tensely through cracks in the silo as they made their way and saw them hesitate in front of the first house they came to in the village.

"They must be afraid to knock," Mother said, perspiration pouring off her forehead and every limb of her body trembling. "I am going to bring them back. I won't let them be in such terrible danger."

But before she could move, we saw the door of the house open and a woman in peasant dress come out and talk to Rachel and Miriam. Then they all entered the house. Soon after — though to us it seemed a very long time — the three of them reappeared and started walking toward the village, away from us. It looked like a bad sign: Where was she taking them? We mustn't abandon them — we have to go after them! But before we could set out, we saw them enter a neighboring house and come out soon afterward carrying a basket. They pointed in our direction, waved goodbye, and began walking toward our hiding place. What a relief! We knew they had succeeded. We waited impatiently to hear their story.

Rachel and Miriam entered the silo smiling broadly, placed the basket on the ground, and said they had brought a true feast: bread, cheese, some carrots, and even dried meat. We happily wolfed down this unexpected bounty. As we ate, we peppered them with questions. Rachel told the story:

"We went up to the first house but we were ashamed to go in. We didn't have any idea how to go about asking for food. What would we tell the people in the house? Would they be good or bad people? Then, luckily for us, a woman came out, even though we didn't knock on the door, and asked us what we wanted. I told her we were looking for a family that had promised to give us food—that was just something I made up on the spot. The woman said, 'I can give you something to eat, too.' Then she looked us over from head to foot and said, 'Isn't it true that you are Jewish girls who escaped from the terrible transports? But where are your parents? And where are you hiding?' We were afraid that maybe the woman would take us to the police, but it was too late to go back.

"We told her that we are Jewish girls who are with our parents in the underground, afraid and hungry. We said that our parents and our big sister are not healthy and need help. The woman took us into her house and gave us hot soup and sausage. She didn't have any more food to give for our family, so she took us to one of the neighbors, a young couple with a girl. She asked them to help these poor girls. The couple gave us a little food, which they put into this basket, and they promised to help us with more food later."

From that fateful day on, the Tokoly family — the family that promised to help — became part of our lives and played a large part in our survival. These generous and kind-hearted people said they would do whatever they could and would not take money, even though their own economic situation was very bad. They promised my sisters that they would collect food from friends and neighbors and soon bring it to us, so we wouldn't have to go into the village and risk being seen by wicked people.

And in fact, soon after Rachel and Miriam returned, Vincent Tokoly arrived at the silo and introduced himself. He was a young man, about 30 years old, tall and thin, and had a noble bearing. He said he would help us. He told us that other Jews were also hiding in the village and that many of the local people were helping them, including the priest, the spiritual father of the community. Vincent's brother, Pavel, was assisting three young Jews who were hiding in one of the huts near us. Vincent suggested that we meet them and then we wouldn't feel so lonely and it would be easier to get through these bad times.

So, with Vincent as the middleman, we arrived toward evening at the hut of the three youths. Two of them were brothers, 16 and 17 years old, and the third was 19. They had gone through a very hard time. The brothers turned out to be from a town close to Michalovce, where I was born, and Father knew the family. The boys' parents had been taken at the very beginning of the deportations, in 1942, but the two brothers had escaped. They had worked here and there in pick-up jobs, wandering through Slovakia and posing as non-Jews with the help of false papers (Luckily for them, their fair features did not arouse suspicion). They had met Jan, the older boy, in 1944, at a shoemaking workshop in the district capital, which was close to Jarok, the village where we were now.

The three held us spellbound with their amazing story. The owner of the workshop was a Jewish woman who had converted to Christianity before the Holocaust, when she married a Christian, so she did not face deportation. In contrast to Germany, couples in mixed marriages here did not suffer from the anti-Jewish decrees during most of the war. Then, toward the end, when no more exceptions were allowed and all the privileged and wealthy began to be arrested, the woman was somehow "forgotten" and her name did not appear on the lists of converts to Christianity who were deported.

In this critical period, when identity documents were checked much more closely, the three boys found themselves in a very precarious situation. The good-hearted woman who owned the workshop advised them to go into hiding; she gave them money and sent them here, to Vincent's brother, Pavel. She and Pavel had business ties going back many years and had become fast friends. The plan was for him to hide the three boys in his house, with the woman to pay for all their needs. However, Pavel's modest home proved to be too small. Pavel had a large family, and it would be too much of a burden to add three teenagers who would have to spend all their time inside the small house. So a few days later he took them to a hut he owned in the area of the silos. He brought them food every day or two and in the evening they went outside for some fresh air. Every once in a while, they came to Pavel's house at night to wash.

We stayed with the boys until it grew dark. The conversation flowed, we told one another our experiences and exchanged views. We decided to meet and talk again, to help relieve the constant tension and pass the time. In the days that followed, the three boys came to our silo every morning and stayed the whole day, until evening. The days were growing shorter and chillier, and at night the cold and the damp penetrated through the cracks in the wall. Winter was fast approaching and the thought of the icy winds and snow made us very anxious.

One day, when Father returned from his forays—which left Mother a bundle of nerves while he was away—he told us that he had almost fallen into a pit in the field, which he hadn't noticed before because it was covered by a dense growth of weeds. He looked more closely and found a wide opening, which was easy to enter. With a pocket flashlight given to him by Vincent, which he always took with him when he went out, he discovered a convenient way to enter the pit through a kind of diagonal corridor. Curious, he crawled inside and found himself fairly deep underground in a large, warm space.

Father climbed out of the pit and went on exploring. He soon found another pit, very much like the first. Then he discovered three more pits, not far from one another. Immediately the idea came to him that we might be able to live in these pits and so get through winter and not be discovered. The three boys, who by now were almost part of the family, liked the idea. We didn't know what the pits were for—after all, someone had dug them, and now they were empty. What was their purpose and who owned them?

Our questions were answered when Vincent paid his next visit. Many years ago, he said, when he was a boy, there was a vineyard here, where wheat was now grown. Some of the families dug cellars for the barrels of new wine, so they would ferment in dry conditions. Years later, they would bring out the barrels and sell the wine. After decades in which the vintners diligently tended the vineyards and made wine, a curse had fallen on them: a drought that lasted for two successive seasons. The vines dried up and could not be revived. They had to uproot the vineyards and instead planted grain. They built silos to store the harvest and for marketing the produce. Eventually all the wine barrels were removed and the cellars had remained unused for many years. There were a few dozen of them, of different sizes, some of which were below the silos themselves.

Vincent agreed that it would be a good idea to make one of the pits a hiding place. He promised to stay in touch with us and bring us a knapsack with food once or twice a week. His brother, Pavel, would continue to bring the boys food that was being paid for by the owner of the shoe workshop.

That very day, we left the cold, leaky silo and, with Vincent's help, found a "cellar" that was relatively spacious and had straight walls. We brought straw from the silo and prepared places to sleep for all of us, and then moved in with the three boys. It was totally dark, because we closed the top by placing boards in a criss-cross pattern, with tiny spaces between them to allow air in, and we scattered straw on the boards as camouflage. We didn't imagine that this hole, which was fitting for mice or other nocturnal animals, would be our home for months. It was the beginning of October 1944, and a lengthy chapter in our lives loomed before us.

Life Underground

Every so often, when the stench became intolerable or the cellar grew moldy, we moved to a different underground "home," which we called "the pit." Life in the pit was crowded and marked by friction, tension, pain, sickness, fear and filth. Still, despite the humiliating circumstances, we felt like an extended family that was sharing a common fate, and that gave us a sense of security. We set up a daily schedule that included, besides meals (Vincent brought us food regularly), bringing water from a spring and "intellectual" activity. For example, each of us in turn would tell a story we remembered from past reading. Only little Miriam was left out, as she had barely begun to enjoy children's literature before our wanderings began. I remember telling parts from "The Heart" by Edmondo de Amicis, and others related what they recalled from "The Count of Monte Christo" and "The Three Musketeers" by Dumas, and also from Jules Verne and Karl May, stories from the Bible—this was mainly Father—and from other books for young people.

We also played group games, taught one another songs we knew, especially songs from the Land of Israel, and described interesting experiences from our own lives. All this was done in total darkness, as we sat or lay on the ground. The only time we lit the kerosene lamp was during meals.

We spoke in Slovakian, which meant that Mother spent most of the time in silence, as she was not fluent in that language. What did she feel? What did she think about during those hours and days in which she was mute? At the time, no one gave this any thought: She was simply outside our circle. She must have suffered terrible loneliness. Once in a long while, she would tell something interesting in Hungarian, which everyone more or less understood.

As for the three boys, besides getting food from Pavel, they continued to go to his house every so often in order to wash. We only had the spring, and sometimes we washed in it—only our hands and face, of course, because it was too cold for more, and anyway there was no way to ensure privacy. Our clothes were filthy, even though Mother occasionally washed them in the spring. Sometimes the clothes stayed damp for days afterward, because they couldn't dry properly in the pit. Soon we all started to itch all over, from flea bites—the fleas thrived in this dirty, warm environment. We played a strange game: By the light of the kerosene lamp we amused ourselves by catching fleas that leaped about on us. We crushed them with our fingernails, listening to the crunch and watching as the blood they had sucked from us flowed out. But despite all our efforts, they kept multiplying and tormenting us.

I was well into puberty, having turned 14 before we went underground, and I had my first menstruation. There, in those unbearable conditions, came the unwanted guest. I felt strong pains in my stomach and blood began to ooze from my lower body. Mother and I didn't know what to do: How to absorb the blood? We had a few shirts and Mother decided to tear one of hers into strips, which I placed inside my underclothes. I felt miserable, ashamed, dirty, polluted. I was especially afraid that the boys would realize what was going on. At the first opportunity, I went with Mother to wash at the spring. The cold water made me shiver and hurt as though I had been sliced open with a sharp knife. The next time our benefactor Vincent arrived with the food, we asked him to bring a few rags from his house, though without explaining why. That traumatic event in the pit below the ground returned to haunt me every month for many years. The frustration and distress were engraved in my memory.

A far more pleasant memory is the day on which the three boys told me that they had decided to ask me to be their girlfriend. But which of them would be my "private" boyfriend? They held a lottery and the winner was the youngest of the group, whom I will call Ronny. If I agreed, he would be my personal boyfriend and I could share my secrets with him. The truth is that from the moment we met the boys I liked Ronny the best, maybe because of his silence, his seriousness, his maturity—and his clear, blue eyes. He intrigued me from the start and I was happy he had won the drawing. Smiling with embarrassment, I agreed to be his girlfriend. Thus began an episode of pure youthful love, my first love affair, which developed and flourished and filled the wretched days in the isolated, dark pit with substance, emotion and beauty.

From that day on, Ronny and I were the regular team that brought water from the spring. During the daily story-telling period, we tried to lie next to each other. The physical closeness that was forced on us by the dark pit brought us close together emotionally. Sometimes I felt his body press against me, his hand searching for my hand, caressing my face. In the absolute dark, we could cuddle up and whisper words of delight. Ronny was quiet by nature, but expressed his love at great length by quoting from the high literature of the many books he had read. When his turn came to tell a story, he remembered the plot in great detail and seemed to be reading the original text and not speaking from memory. We listed to his stories with great interest and curiosity, and he riveted us with his powers of description.

During the months in which we were together, Ronny and I grew constantly closer. Our young hearts overflowed with the experience of falling in love. We forgot where we were; we were immersed within ourselves, daydreaming and excited by the discovery of thrills that were completely new to us. The otherwise stagnant life below ground became more tolerable. The two other boys knew about our relationship; even if we had wanted to hide it from them, it would have been impossible in the conditions of the pit. They probably envied us, too, but our friendship and the sense of a common fate were not affected. Mother and Father, though, knew nothing. The two of us lived in a magic bubble and everything outside it passed over us and left us untouched. We promised each other that if we survived, we would never part and would be a couple for all time.

Ronny was shy and hesitant. Every once in a while he came so close that I could feel his warm breath. We were face to face and my heart pounded with expectation, but it always ended with nothing more than holding hands. Until one day we moved closer and closer, we almost stopped breathing, and our lips almost touched. I felt myself quivering and waiting, my whole body was flooded with warmth as he came even closer. His lips touched mine gently. Soft lips, searching, shy. The first kiss! What happiness, what sweetness. When we broke apart, I felt embarrassed and confused, but I wanted his lips again. Our trembling lips came together and we held our breath, as though to perpetuate the moment. From that instant, we entered into a pact of secret love. We made whispered plans for the future.

"Grandmother, so how come you married Grandfather and not that Ronny? Where is he now? Are you still friends with him?" Omer asked.

"You're right to ask, Omer. I will get ahead of myself in the story and answer your questions," I said. "When the liberation finally arrived—not before we went through many more ordeals, which I will soon tell you about—and we came out of the darkness into the light, I saw our relationship differently. I went back to being a girl who wasn't yet 15, a student who had to make up for lost time in her studies—I had missed so much during the war years, you know. New people and things came into my life. The light outside the dark 'pit,' where we had lived in intimacy, changed the way I felt about our relationship and took me in different directions. The

*period of running and hiding, with all its fears, was over, and
so was the closeness and the dependence between us. We each
went our separate ways in mutual agreement and friendship.*

*"Ronny and his brother came to Israel right after the war.
My family and I arrived two years later. Ronny's brother was
killed in the War of Independence and he was left all alone in
the world, as his whole family perished in the Holocaust.
Today he is married and has children and grandchildren; he
lives on a kibbutz of which he was one of the founders and is
happy and content. We remained in touch after we came to
Israel and even after we both had our own families.*

*"When we met, which was not very often, we would
remember emotionally our beautiful and naive friendship.
The wonderful and special relationship we developed in that
pit remains etched in my heart. We knew that our puppy love
in the depths of the earth was the only beautiful episode in that
time and that it gave us strength and resilience to cope with
our desperate plight. The relationship we forged helped us to
overcome the reality around us, to keep our hopes up, and to
let us believe that we would live."*

The dreary routine of the pit dulled our senses and lessened
our vigilance. Occasionally, before dark, Father would
leave the pit—"to get a bit of air," he said—and leave us
anxious until he returned. One day he informed us that it
was the first day of the new Jewish month (he must have
known this from watching the moon on the nights before),
so he intended to go out in broad daylight and recite the
prayer for the occasion beneath the open skies and not
in the dirty and polluted pit. He crawled out on the

diagonal ramp, covered the entrance with the boards and disappeared.

He was gone for a very long time and we began to be concerned, especially Mother, who was almost hysterical. Finally we heard the familiar sound of the boards and straw being moved up top, and in the light that penetrated the darkness of the pit we saw Father. We all sighed with relief. But then Father told us a frightening story about what had kept him. He encountered two *gardists* who had wanted to take him with them. Father had no money, so he offered his expensive Omega watch as a bribe. The two greedily grabbed the treasure and made off. Father thought they had only pretended to be *gardists*, otherwise they wouldn't have let him go. Even so, there was a good chance they would have turned him in. Father became agitated when he mentioned that possibility, but he was happy he had made it back. Mother made him swear never to go outside again in daylight.

The first day of the week was always special, as Vincent would appear carrying a knapsack filled with food. Sometimes he also brought hot soup in a pot, usually rabbit soup, and his young wife, Anna, also joined him frequently. We knew it was them when we heard the special whistle we had agreed on as a signal. They sat with us as we lay in a row side by side, and they brought a fresh breeze of hope and sanity from another world. Their reports about the Allies' advance and the Germans' certain defeat gave us strength to go on enduring the stagnant life that had been forced on us. Vincent would show us with pleasure the treasures he had collected for us: a large, round bread with a

My mother's parents: Grandfather Mordechai
and Grandmother Esther with the
grandchildren

My father's parents: Grandfather Natan and
Grandmother Ruhama

Grandmother Esther with her daughters Zipora
(Olga) and Ilonka, and the grandchildren

My parents, Moshe and Zipora, Michalovce,
winter 1940

Aliza at the age of two

Aliza at the age of three with her sister, Rachel, aged one

Aliza in the school choir, Michalovce, 1940

Purim party in the Jewish school at Michalovce, 1940

The teaching staff in the school at Michalovce

Aliza, Miriam, and the cousins, Budapest, 1943

The Great Synagogue in Michalovce

A memorial plaque for the 4,000 Jews of Michalovce who perished in the Holocaust

Anna Tokoly, the Slovakian woman from the village of Jarok, who with her husband saved the family, 1946

The certificate presented by Yad Vashem to Vincent and Anna Tokoly

Aliza and Rachel at Mikveh Yisrael, 1947

The Ressler family shortly after their arrival in Israel

Aliza, 1947

Aliza and her husband Avigdor with their
children Eli, Gadi, and Lior

The three sisters — Aliza, Rachel, and Miriam
— meet with the daughter of Vincent and
Anna, Jarok, 1990

The grandchildren

tempting aroma, baked goods and high-quality pork or sausage. We accepted the fine food he brought gratefully. With great satisfaction, we heard him say that every Sunday during Mass, the priest hinted openly and clearly in his sermon that it was the duty of the congregation to assist those who were in grave distress, be it material or spiritual.

"It is wrong to hate anyone for his religion, his opinions or his different customs, for we have all been created by God," the priest said. With that noble declaration, this special clergyman joined those who took an active part in rescuing us and providing for our needs. As we ate the excellent food that the priest sent us—except for Father, of course, who would not even touch anything that was not kosher—we felt strengthened by the knowledge that we had a patron in the village who was protecting us.

There were too few examples of greatness of spirit and humane deeds in Slovakia during the war, including among members of the clergy, in contrast to the exemplary behavior of the priest in Jarok. We were also told that the priest, whom the villagers called a "saint," was a freedom fighter and a great humanist who had been a senior member of the Catholic Church establishment. However, when he openly protested the persecution of the Jews and denounced the regime, he was punished by being exiled to this little village. Fortunately for us, he was not harmed physically and was not sent to a concentration camp—but only because President Tiso, who collaborated with Nazis, was also a clergyman, as I have already mentioned, and had been at school with this special priest. The President remembered those old times and gave him his protection.

The days passed with monotonous sameness. Again we decided that the time had come to move to a new and cleaner pit. A night search turned up a fairly large cellar, which seemed to be large enough for our needs. We usually moved to a new site when the stench from our excretions—which we only emptied out after dark—became absolutely unbearable. Sometimes we weren't able to find a large enough pit and we had to stay put.

One day in November, Pavel, Vincent's brother, who was still bringing food to the three boys, suggested that I join his daughter Clara, who was 16, on her trip to town to meet with the Jewish woman and receive the monthly payment for the boys' food. Father and Mother objected, saying it was too dangerous. A heated argument broke out, until finally they gave in with a heavy heart, though only after hearing the details of the plan. I would dress like a peasant girl, with clothes I would get from Clara, and go into town with her using public transportation.

Very excited, I said goodbye to everyone. I was delighted to have been chosen for a mission that meant I would be free, out of the pit, for one day, at least. I emerged from the bowels of the earth and Pavel accompanied me to the village. We reached the house safely. Clara, whom I had already met, had prepared a tub of hot water for me to wash in. That was a celebration in itself—I couldn't remember the last time I had washed myself like a human being. The colorful peasant clothes I was to wear were laid out on a chair. After the refreshing bath, Clara helped me put on the many skirts, the embroidered blouse and the kerchief. I hardly recognized myself in the small mirror on the wall.

We both smiled happily and, arm in arm, set out on our adventure.

I walked along the street with mixed feelings of fear and happiness. No one paid attention to us as we made our way to the village's one bus stop. We looked like two ordinary girls. On the way we went into a church, as Clara wanted to ask the Virgin Mary to protect us from harm and help us fulfill our mission. We entered a large hall. Across the way was a statue of the Virgin, and candles were burning on a table. The only other person there was an old woman who was kneeling and mumbling prayers. Clara lit a candle and also went down on her knees, indicating to me to do the same. I hesitated and continued to stand, but she urged me firmly to do as she did; and, having no choice, I did. I muttered a few meaningless words and sounds and recited the Ave Maria, which I remembered from school. I felt my conscience tugging at me as we left the church, as though I had betrayed the God of Israel. My heart started to pound as two men in uniform passed us on the street, but they smiled brightly at us and walked on. Encouraged, we boarded the bus.

The trip to the town of Nitra took about an hour. I had the feeling that everyone was staring at me and that they all knew exactly who I was. For sure a policeman would suddenly appear and arrest me. But Clara whispered to me that everything was going normally and that there was nothing to be afraid of: I looked just like her. It was quite chilly—there was no heating in public buses in those days—and I trembled with cold in the light peasant clothing, or maybe it was from the tension and anxiety I felt. We came to Nitra, from which I had fled with my family more than two months ago. As we walked toward the town center, I looked at the people on the street. How strange it was to see people walking about freely, talking calmly and laughing with pleasure! Children scampered about—everything seemed perfectly normal. I felt as though I were floating in a dream. Were we living in the same world? Was this the reality and was life in the pit the dream?

In the woman's workshop, men and women sat in a row, each hunched over a sewing machine, which they used to assemble shoes from the material in front of them. They used a foot pedal to work the machines. A dull noise filled the room.

The owner, a handsome woman of about 35, welcomed Clara like an old friend. She took us to her apartment, which was attached to the workshop in the rear of the building. Clara introduced me and I explained my family's connection with the three boys whom she was supporting. She stuffed some money into my hand, too, and with downcast eyes hinted that within a short time she might no longer be protected against deportation. There were rumors that even the longtime converts to Christianity were going to be treated like Jews. However, she declared, she would go on supporting the boys, who had once worked for her, as long as she could, and perhaps God would reward her by looking after her and her family. We had something to eat and drink in her house and then she gave Clara the monthly payment for the boys, wrapped in a napkin. We said goodbye and set out for home.

Now I felt more liberated and confident as I walked along the busy street. It was a powerful experience to feel free, without having to wear a yellow patch, and to imagine that everything would work out for the best. For many days after returning to the pit, I summoned up that feeling and longed for the day when the nightmare of our life underground would end.

The old routine continued. It was impossible to tell day from night in the pit and the time there seemed to stretch endlessly. Then, one Sunday, Father crawled up to the edge of the pit, felt the warm sun, and suggested that we all come out to get some fresh air without waiting for nightfall. Most of the village people were in church or at home with their families on Sunday, Father said; they didn't work in the fields, so we could take it almost for granted that the area would be "clean." The desire to see the light of day and just to be outside after more than a month in the pit overcame our hesitations and our good judgment. We followed Father out, shook the dust and dirt from our clothes, and waited for the boys to follow, but they said they would stay below and go out as a group when we came back.

Savoring our freedom and drinking in the fresh air, we walked a little distance from the pit in order to stretch our legs. Father was in front and we followed. Then, with no warning at all, two men wearing the uniform of the Hlinka Guard suddenly appeared.

We froze. We all had the same thought: Because of a momentary lapse of judgment, all our efforts and all the ploys we had used to survive would come to nothing. All our attempts to survive had been useless. Without unnecessary talk, the two signaled us to accompany them to the village. Father searched his pockets and offered them what money he still had. They took the money but didn't seem about to let us go. Then something totally unexpected happened, something we had never planned or even talked about—maybe because we never imagined that it was possible.

Miriam, my little sister, who was eight and a half, got on her knees, embraced the leg of one of the men, broke into tears and begged, "Please, I am still little, I want to live, let us go, let us go free!"

Stunned by Miriam's amazing initiative, all we could do was gape at her. But there was another surprise yet to come. The man whose leg Miriam embraced did not kick her, did not shake her off, did not shout at her and did not hit her. He too was stunned and moved. His eyes filled with tears as he bent over and picked up Miriam, stood her on her feet and said, "Go, run away, fast!"

His comrade stared at him and at us as though not believing his eyes and ears. We could hardly believe it either. But the other man did nothing. They both turned away and walked toward the village.

We stood there for another moment, too astonished at Miriam's courageous behavior to move. Despite her young age, she had touched the hearts of these guards who held our fate in their hands. It took us a few minutes to recover from the shock we had experienced, and then we returned quickly, almost running, to our warm and "safe" pit.

Then came a truly shocking incident that proved decisive. We were lying down, as usual, when suddenly we heard a noise from the opening above. We knew it wasn't Vincent or Pavel, because there was no identifying signal. We hardly dared breathe. We heard vague sounds of talking and shivers ran through us: They were speaking German. Father signaled to us to stand up against the wall and not to budge, leaving the center of the floor empty in case anyone looked below. He placed his hand over Miriam's mouth to make sure she didn't cry or scream. I stood against the wall. Next to me, Ronny's brother held my hand. His palm was sweating and I could sense his whole body shaking with fear. My heart pounded wildly, my stomach heaved, I felt like throwing up.

The people above us pushed aside the straw and the boards, and a faint light entered the cellar. Suddenly there was a tremendous crack. It was a rifle shot. There was a flash of light and a bullet plunged into the earth in the center of the floor. The Germans shouted "*Raus! Raus!*" — "Out! Out!" — but we were rooted to the spot like mute statues. Another shot rang out and then another and yet another. The bullets whistled by our ears and slammed into the ground by our feet. We were horror-stricken, utterly aghast, completely paralyzed — and that was what probably stopped us from simply surrendering to the Germans and ending the terrible nightmare.

We heard some more vague sounds of talking, then silence and suddenly another burst of gunfire, the bullets grazing Father's shoe. He must have been horribly shaken, but he did not react. We were in a state of shock, totally silent, showing no sign of life. I don't remember how long this terror lasted, but finally a heavy silence fell. The voices above faded away until there was total quiet once more. We were all shaking uncontrollably, crying and gasping for breath. But when we pulled ourselves together we knew we had to make a decision: certainly we had to move to another cellar.

Later that same day, Vincent arrived in great agitation and told us that someone in the village must have informed the Germans about us because they had suddenly arrived and immediately gone to the area of the pits in order to root out the people in hiding there. They found one group of Jews and took them away. They might come back, Vincent said, and next time they might throw grenades into the pits from which steam arose or that smelled of human habitation. We told Vincent about our own traumatic experience and asked him why the Germans hadn't entered the cellar if they suspected people were hiding there. He said they might have been afraid because of reports they had received that armed partisans were hiding in the cellars, so the soldiers might be risking their lives by going below.

We discussed what to do and finally decided that we should leave the area for a few days until things calmed down again. Father suggested that we return to the village of Cabaj-Čapor, to Jozef, at whose home we had stayed for more than a week. The boys were very depressed at the idea that we would split up, though we knew we would not leave them behind. Our time in the pit together had made us one family. We told Vincent that we would leave that very night and that with God's help, if all went well, we would be back soon.

By now the days were very short and darkness fell early, so we were able to leave almost immediately. Once again, as we left a place that had been "home" and set out for the unknown, I seemed to be choking and felt a crushing anxiety. Would we find Jozef? Would he agree to take in eight people? But there was no other choice, and all we could do was try our luck and hope for the best. I had lost count of how many times we had taken our few belongings and stolen away under cover of dark—this time heading for the village we had left two months ago or more.

It was freezing cold. As we walked, I remembered the seemingly endless trek of a year ago, when my sister and I crossed the border into Hungary. Now everything seemed to be repeating itself. We were all terribly on edge. No one said a word. Ronny stayed close to me, squeezing my hand every once in a while to cheer me up. The moon cast a pale light on the fields. Little Miriam was the only one who didn't have to walk—the boys took turns carrying her on their shoulders. Our feet hurt, but we kept going until, after a few hours, we saw the lights of the village.

We knocked on Jozef's door. He gasped in surprise to see us and told us to come in at once. After we got our breath back, we told him about our plight and asked if he would help us again. He said we could all stay and again offered us the big bed on which we had slept last time. We smiled in embarrassment. Could eight people sleep in one bed, even if it was a wide bed? We experimented by lying down next to one another in our clothes—it was so crowded we could only lie on our side—and we laughed and said now we knew what it was like to be sardines in a can. Naturally, it was impossible to sleep like that. In the end, our family slept on the bed and we made a place for the boys on the floor.

Father still had a little money left and he gave half of it to the peasant. The boys also took out some of the money they had received from the woman and gave it to Jozef. He took the money without counting it and went to the barn to organize the sleeping quarters for his family. I went with Father to help him. In the barn we saw piles of grain and a cow standing in the middle of the floor. We moved the cow aside and arranged a place on which they could sleep. When we got back to the house, Mother and the girls were already curled up under the down quilt and we lay down beside them, pulling the quilt over us, too. We had no idea what the next day would bring, but we fell asleep almost at once, exhausted, without giving any more thought to the future.

The Betrayal

After a deep, dreamless sleep, I awoke very early in the morning, while it was still dark, to the first day of our new stay in the village of Cabaj-Čapor. It took me a bit of time to remember where I was — we had changed places so many times during our long wandering. But early as it was, Mother and Father were already up and the boys' improvised bed on the floor was gone. They were all huddled in the dark outside; only my two little sisters still slept, and now they had the whole big bed to themselves.

I looked around the room, which hadn't changed since we were last here. In the corner, Jozef's wife was bent over the stove, feeding it with logs. I watched as she went about her tasks very efficiently. She took a jug of milk from the shelf on the wall and placed it on the stove to heat up and then took a large round bread and began slicing it. She soon added a jar of home made jam and set the table.

After eating heartily — I was so hungry that it almost hurt — I looked out the window. There was a curtain, so I could look out without being afraid that someone could see in from the outside. The houses of the village stood side by side in rows. Only Jozef's house stood apart from the rest—which was excellent, as no prying eyes could get a good look at us. Still, I asked myself, are we really safe in this house, our haven for a second time?

Jozef prepared food for us, consisting mainly of milk, bread and potatoes, and promised rabbit stew for the weekend. There was very little to eat, and we distributed it twice a day, making sure that everyone got their proper share. The first day passed quietly but nervously. In the evening,we went out to the courtyard to get some air. It was cold and we didn't have the right clothes for the approaching winter. Another day passed—of which I remember very little, as the time went by so slowly—and we tried to find something to occupy ourselves with.

On the third day, Jozef came up with a surprising suggestion. The house wasn't safe enough, he said, and we should prepare a place to hide in case of an emergency. With the help of the four men—Father and the three boys—he was ready to help build a secret hiding place in the barn. One of the men would sneak out to the barn every day and together with Jozef would help build a small underground room, a kind of cellar, where we would be able to hide for a long time in case of danger. They would dig during the day, with one of us standing guard to warn of approaching trouble. The earth from the digging would be loaded onto the cart and scattered in the garden. When the cellar was large enough, a long bench would be placed in it for us to sit on and the entrance would be covered with boards, which would be hidden by straw. To be on the safe side, the cow would be made to stand on the boards and straw that formed the roof of the cellar—that would be its permanent place. No one would think that there was a space beneath the cow where people were hiding.

We thanked Jozef for his concern and agreed to his suggestion. Father and the boys went to work and we saw them from time to time through the door, which was opposite the barn. The ground was hard and the work went slowly and wore them all out; at the end of the day they were exhausted and had blisters on their hands. Still, despite their poor physical condition, the lack of basic necessities, and above all the fact that there was not enough nourishing food, the work was done in a week. The little room was ready, the work of our men, who were delighted and very proud of what they had accomplished. Jozef then brought a long bench, which we all helped to haul into the new pit, and toward evening we crawled down into the cellar to see what it would feel like with the eight of us there. We sat down on the bench and decided that the next day we would practice going down into the shelter as quickly as possible. We also decided who would go first and last. The more we practiced, the faster we became at rushing down into the cellar; coming up was harder and slower, and we helped one another.

Father had another worry on his mind. Our money and the boys' money, too, was fast running out. What would happen in another day or two, when we could no longer pay the peasant? Father hinted to him that we might have to send someone to the city to get cash, referring to the woman who helped the boys. It was obvious that Jozef didn't like the idea, but he said nothing.

Two days had passed since we finished digging. It was

Friday, and Jozef suggested that we take advantage of the good weather to wash our dirty clothes. His wife did laundry every Saturday, he said, and she would do our things too. On Saturday morning the woman lit a fire beneath a vat that stood in the courtyard, occasionally adding logs to keep the blaze going and the water hot. She washed the clothes in a large pail of boiling water overflowing with soap suds. With one hand she held a square surface made of corrugated metal, on which she rubbed each item of clothing in a downward motion. I watched as though in a trance as her hands moved at a steady pace, untiringly, and steam rose from the pail and fogged her face. I remember that she even asked Miriam for her doll—she undressed it and then washed its clothes as well. Within a few hours our things were hanging on the lines to dry in the sun and wind.

The next morning, as the ringing of the church bells echoed in our ears, taking me back in my memory to that other church two years before, and before we had a chance to eat, Jozef came rushing into the room and with frightened gestures and a high-pitched voice told us to go down to the shelter as fast as we could. They were searching the village for people who had fled, he said, and he was afraid the troops would come here, too.

We rushed to the barn, pushed the cow aside, cleared the straw and the boards, and went down into the cellar and sat on the bench, just as we had practiced. Jozef quickly covered up the entrance and moved the cow back to its position above us. We sat in tense silence for about ten minutes, and then something terribly embarrassing happened. The cow relieved itself and some of the urine came down through the cracks and splashed onto us. If we hadn't been so anxious, we would have burst out laughing — or crying. We tried to move our heads to keep out of the range of the urine, but we kept silent. When would we finally get the "all clear" signal so we could come out?

Suddenly we heard voices. People were shouting and pounding. Then came the terrible words: Someone was shouting at Jozef to open the barn. The door opened and the footsteps came closer to our ceiling. There was pounding on the floor of the barn, until finally it reached the boards above us. Jozef was told to move the cow and the pounding continued until it produced a hollow sound. Then Jozef was ordered to remove the straw, revealing the boards, which made it obvious that there was a cellar below.

We were mesmerized. Light began to penetrate our dark abode. We trembled with fear and helplessness. Ronny held my hand and whispered, "You'll see, we'll get out of this, God won't let a love like ours end." The words hurtled into me as though from a different reality and nestled in my heart; I became totally wrapped up in myself and hardly took in what was about to happen. A kind of calm acceptance gripped me, which hardly suited the situation. Even today, more than 55 years later, I can see myself sitting there on that bench, holding Ronny's hand and hearing his exact words — words that made such a powerful impression on me!

After the boards were cleared away, we were ordered to come out of the cellar. Father went ahead of me and helped me out. Three young men in uniforms of the *gardists* burst out laughing when they saw us: "Look at the miserable wretches. The cow pissed on them!"

Mother worked up her courage and went over to one of them. "I am a Christian," she said, speaking German. "We were escaping from the bombings."

But the man screamed at her: "Stinking Jewess! How do you dare tell us those stupid lies!"

He raised his hand and slapped Mother across the face with all his might. Then he grabbed her by the ear and ripped off an earring. Blood spurted out of her earlobe. Mother collapsed onto the floor howling with pain and we girls started crying. Father stood there, pale and petrified, not reacting. The man who struck Mother shouted at us to stop crying, otherwise he would hit us, too. I thought that now the peasant would also be punished for helping us.

But to my surprise, one of the *gardists* whispered something in his ear and patted him on the shoulder. Suddenly the naked truth became clear and threw me into utter despair: The man had betrayed us! When he discovered that we had no more money, he informed on us to the police. The troops told us to hurry. We helped Mother up; she had blood on her and was weeping softly. One of the *gardists* announced that the bus was about to leave from the village and that we had to go with them immediately.

They didn't even give us time to collect our clothes, which were still hanging on the line, not yet dry. Now I realized that washing our clothes was part of the scheme that aimed to rob us of all we had. When little Miriam asked for her doll, she was told that no one knew where it was. (By the way, after the war, we came back to the village to demand the doll, to which Miriam was very attached. We found it without its legs and with its face squashed by the couple's boy. Nevertheless, Miriam insisted on taking the doll; it is now in the collection of the Yad Vashem Museum).

We went out into the cold without proper clothes for the winter, the rest of our clothes having been taken by fraud. Heads bent, we marched toward the bus station in the center of the village. People watched through their windows and their looks seemed to stab us. The bus was jammed. The policemen got on with us and we all stood. One of the passengers wanted to give his seat to Mother, who held a bloodied handkerchief which she placed on her torn ear every so often. However, the cruel policeman who had injured her told the passenger, "Don't bother. They are only Jews who escaped from the law. There is no reason to give up your place for them."

Their discomfiture obvious, people averted their eyes and said nothing. One of the *gardists*, the youngest of the three, stood next to me and I saw what seemed to be embarrassment in his eyes, as though he was ashamed of what had happened. I gathered all my courage and whispered to him, "What did we do to you that you are so cruel to us? Aren't we human beings who were created in God's image like you?"

He mumbled something and I thought I heard, "I'm only obeying orders, it's my job."

The trip took about an hour. Finally we reached Nitra, from which we had set out more than three months earlier, though it seemed much longer because so much had happened since then. We had gone through so many ordeals: days of fear, grief, suffering, and endless wandering, broken only by rare moments of hope and joy. Was this the end of our desperate attempt to survive? Would all our efforts and stratagems to escape and hide and somehow get along until the storm passed come to nothing? I had no idea where we were being taken or what would happen to us. While we were still on the bus, Mother whispered to me that I should ask the young policeman for permission to go to our apartment and get warm clothing. It took me time to work up the courage to make the request, and I was amazed to get a positive reply — the *gardists* agreed to let us enter our house, which was in fact on the road leading to the district prison, where Jews were sent before being deported.

The freezing cold lashed at us again as we got off the bus. We started walking toward the prison and soon came to the house we had lived in before fleeing into the forest. The policemen removed the wax seal, opened the lock, and said Father and I could go in, escorted by one of them, in order to pick up clothing. As I entered, I was gripped by the familiar choking feeling and a tremendous weakness overcame me — I almost collapsed from the surge of emotion. Once I lived in this house! Father quickly collected a few coats and a down quilt and wrapped some things in small parcels. Outside, each of us dressed warmly and began the walk to the prison, carrying a small parcel.

We walked with heads bowed through streets we knew so well and soon came to a tall building. On one floor there was a movie theater, and the others were used for government offices and for the headquarters of the Germans and the Hlinka Guard. There was a large basement, containing huge braziers that supplied central heating for the building, along with a few small rooms in which coal was stored. Changes had been made in the basement to turn it into a prison, where Jews from the whole region were held before being deported to the concentration camps. At first, there were almost daily transports. However, as time passed, fewer and fewer people were arrested, so the authorities waited until there were enough Jews to justify sending a train to the East.

Now, in the middle of December 1944, just a few months before the war ended, hardly any Jews remained in Slovakia, so transports were very infrequent. Still, the policemen told us that only the day before there had been a transport to Poland of Jews who were caught hiding in the area. However, when we were taken down to the basement-prison that was to be our new "home," we found only one Jew there, a young man of about 20 named Josef. He said he was sorry we had been caught and that he was afraid we might be sent to Poland after more Jews were rounded up.

When the police left and we were alone, Father suddenly said, in Yiddish: "*Geloibt zim Got, men huben an dach ofen kopf*" (Thank God, now we have a roof over our heads).

That sentence unnerved me. Even if it sounded logical at the moment — we would certainly be protected from the cold here and not have to keep running all the time — it didn't make much sense in the light of what we knew was in store for us. Or perhaps I was simply appalled to hear Father utter such a paradox — as though he was grateful and wanted to thank the Lord for our having been caught and imprisoned. What has happened to Father, who never stops hunting for solutions and stratagems, I asked myself. Has he lost hope? Has he too given up after all our ordeals? Is he ready to submit to the fate of deportation and extermination? Father's surprising remark remained engraved in our collective family memory; we quoted it on suitable occasions, such as when we encountered people who tried to prettify serious situations. Yet at the same time, and this is the strangest thing of all, we quickly adopted the remark in all seriousness and without mockery — an attempt, perhaps, to find the good in any situation, however terrible.

We lay down on the bunk beds that were scattered between the heating pipes. Josef told us that he had been here for a few months because of his profession. As a shoemaker, he had become "friends" with one of the guards, who was only too pleased to have shoes made and repaired, not only for him but for his friends, too. The guard hid Josef before every *Aktion* and transport. Whenever a new batch of Jews was brought to the basement, he was afraid that his turn had come, too, though he always hoped to be spared. He told us that food was provided once a day and that the prisoners had to work shoveling coal into containers.

"Pray that they don't find any more Jews and then they won't take us away," Josef said in good spirits. We asked him what the minimum number of Jews was that had been transported while he was here. He replied that at least 25 to 30 Jews were needed for a transport. The Jews in this prison were combined with another group in a different city and the transport left from there for the East.

At the time, we didn't yet know what a concentration camp meant for children, the weak, and the aged. We had heard contradictory rumors and we preferred to believe soothing lies rather than the frightening truth.

In Prison

It seemed the central prison would be the final stop in our wandering. No longer would we encounter surprises along the way or suffer through days of deep anxiety; no longer would we be constantly on the run—the games of "hide-and-seek" were finally over. We made our peace with this final and irreversible situation. Body and soul were weary after two and a half years of flight, of the relentless search for places to hide, of a life marked by dirt and degradation. A feeling of tranquil acceptance came over us. After our aimless wandering in the forest and our hiding in underground pits, the basement prison offered protection against the cold and the rain. It was also the end of the unknown for us. So, as I said, hard as it is to explain, we adopted Father's paradox.

Each of us was given a narrow, thin mattress. The large braziers scattered around the basement gave off a dense heat, and the air was stale.

Our first information about life in prison came from Josef the shoemaker. The guards not only hid him when there was a transport, they also sometimes brought him far better food than the other prisoners received and even gave him money to buy cigarettes or meat. By now we had nothing, neither money nor anything that was worth money, and the boys were in the same predicament. We were given tiny portions of bland food, which we ate only to stave off hunger.

On our second day in the basement, we began to wander around, especially intrigued by the network of thick pipes that ran across the walls and ceiling and carried heat to the rest of the building. We found a loose brick behind one of the pipes. Father, always curious, removed it, and to our amazement we saw a bulging bag that was tied with string. The bag turned out to contain a large amount of money and an expensive, fancy pocket watch with a long, silver chain attached to it.

It must have been Jews who hid this treasure here before their cruel captors took everything from them, we thought. Probably they hoped to return one day and reclaim their property. We knew it would not be possible to locate the owners and we decided that rather than let the guards find the money, we should use it for our needs. Maybe there were other valuables hidden in the basement, too, but a search turned up nothing more. Still, we were very happy, knowing that we could use the money to improve our conditions. Maybe we too would get better food, and possibly even be able to bribe the guards to keep us from being deported.

Still, the future was uncertain. Were we about to be placed on the next train? We hoped that no more Jews would be arrested, so that we would not be transported — after all, they would not organize a transport for only eight Jews.

In the meantime, the men were put to work loading coal in the storeroom—apart from Josef, who had a corner of his own where he repaired shoes—under the supervision of a guard. After filling containers with coal, they emptied them into the braziers. One wall of the coal cellar was also an outside wall of the building. The coal was piled high, reaching almost to the ceiling. Day by day, the pile grew smaller, until a long, very narrow opening was revealed in this outer wall, beyond which the sidewalk was visible. Each new supply of coal was dumped into the coal cellar through this opening.

Sometimes we girls would join the men and look through the opening at the people on the sidewalk. We could see only their legs, more or less as far as the knees, and we would try to guess, according to the size and style of the shoes or boots, whether a person was an adult or a child, a man or a woman. It was like watching a movie with the top part cut off, a fantasy movie. In fact, the whole world outside the prison looked like a fantasy that had nothing to do with our lives. Across the road we saw railroad cars for transporting coal and other supplies, perhaps also for transporting Jews.

At the end of the workday, the guard had a simple and efficient method of locking the coal cellar. He took a door handle from his pocket, inserted it into the door, then locked the door and removed the handle. This ensured that the door would remain locked until morning. To open the door the next morning, the guard repeated the operation in reverse, this time unlocking the door before placing the handle back in his pocket.

On our third evening in the basement, one of the guards came down and told Mother that the next morning she was to report upstairs in order to clean offices and sort objects left behind by Jews who were sent to the camps. However, when he saw Mother's physical condition (she still suffered terrible earaches from the blow she had taken) and discovered that she was not fluent in the local language, he said the order was canceled. Then he saw me and told me to report upstairs in the morning instead of Mother. He turned and left without waiting for a response. We discussed this development at length. Mother was especially worried: Would I be alone with them? She was afraid that I would come to harm.

It was a chance to leave the moldy, stuffy basement, but I didn't know whether to be happy or sad. "Up there" I would be able to breathe clean air, but the thought of being separated from my family and the boys was frightening. Besides, I didn't think I would be able to do the work, since I had no experience.

The next morning a guard came and told me to follow him upstairs. Mother tried to intervene. Asking us to translate, she explained to the guard that I was only a girl and not fit for the work. But the guard told her to shut up and ordered me to follow him. We walked up a few flights of stairs. Every step took me farther from my family and made my heart pound more strongly. Finally, we left the staircase and entered a large, well-lit hall, where the floor was covered with piles of personal objects of all kinds.

The guard told me to sort the items: clothes in one pile, shoes in another and so on. He warned me not to dare to take anything for myself and said that any money or other valuables I might find must be turned over to one of the guards. At the end of the day I would be searched, he said, and for my own good I must not be tempted into taking a risk and hiding something, because I would be caught and punished severely. As he turned to go, I asked him why people had left their belongings here. He replied that each person was allowed to take up to 20 kilograms of personal effects and that the objects here had been left behind after the weight limit was reached, and had been confiscated "for the benefit of the state."

The guard left, locking the door behind him. I looked at the huge piles and felt terribly sad. With every item of clothing that I picked up, I felt the warmth of the body that had once worn it. And with every object, I wondered who the owner was, what had happened to him, where he was today. When would the time come for our clothes to be sorted, too, and by whom? I sorted the items as I had been ordered and searched the pockets of the coats, trousers, and skirts. I found nothing of value but there were a lot of hankies, some of which I stuffed into my pockets, hoping this would not arouse the guard's suspicion. I was happy to have pieces of cloth to use for my menstrual period, which was due in the next few days. At the end of the day's work, during which no one bothered to bring me food or drink, as though I had been completely forgotten, I was taken back to the basement. Everyone was relieved to see me return safe and sound, and I was given something to eat from their food. I showed mother the treasure I had found and I told the group that no one had searched me or even asked me if I had taken anything. Still, I promised myself that I would not be tempted under any circumstances.

The next morning we followed the same routine. I saw that new items had been added overnight, apparently from other detention centers. I encountered new objects in my sorting activity: purses containing family photographs, make-up, combs and brushes, soap, even bottles of perfume. After such a long period of going without such things, I couldn't resist the temptation and I put lipstick, a comb, and a small bottle of perfume in my pocket. At the end of the day I was paralyzed with fear that I would be searched. I scolded myself for being so stupid and foolish and for endangering myself over such trifles. But again there was no search.

On my third day upstairs I didn't take anything, which was fortunate, because that day I was searched. After that I didn't dare take a thing. Once I even found a wallet with money in it and I handed it over at the end of the day. The guard was pleased—I was certain he took the money for himself.

After a few days of sorting personal belongings, I was sent to a conference hall, where I was to sweep the floor and dust the pictures, shelves and chairs. Among the pictures on the walls I saw portraits of President Tiso and of his predecessor, Hlinka, for whom the Hlinka Guard was named. Of course, there was also a photograph of Hitler. In the center of the front wall of the room hung a large cross with a representation of the crucified Jesus, his face expressing torment. What a satanic combination, I thought to myself: the crucified founder of Christianity, who preached mercy and love, hanging alongside photographs of war criminals who were acting in his name. If Jesus were alive, I thought, he would probably die a second time, from grief, at seeing how his followers had lost any semblance of humanity and had brought disaster to his fellow Jews.

During the days that followed, I worked alternately at sorting and at cleaning. One day, when I returned to the basement after my day's work, I found that, in addition to our extended family, another family had been brought in: parents and two children, a son and daughter around ten years old. They said they had been arrested after being betrayed by the people who had been hiding them, even though they had paid the family a great deal of money. We knew that every addition to the prison increased the risk that we would be deported. A week had already gone by since our arrival here; the days went by calmly enough, though there was a constant fear that more Jews would be arrested until there would be enough to justify a transport to the East.

The Allies sometimes bombed Nitra and we prayed for a bomb to fall on our building, too, even though it would endanger us. It was December 21, 1944. Through the narrow opening to the street from the coal cellar we saw snow piling up outside. We were pleased and took consolation from the fact that at least we weren't outside in the cold. We saw people carrying Christmas trees and even in the basement prison we sensed the hustle and bustle of the holiday preparations, despite the war and the bombing raids.

The next day I was again sent to clean one of the offices.

As I was about to finish sweeping and start dusting the chairs, a guard I had never seen before entered the room and watched me work. He said nothing, only watched. I glanced at him out of the corner of my eye and saw a broad-shouldered, balding, elderly looking man — though maybe he was no more than 40 and only looked old to me. Afraid he would criticize my work, I applied myself to dusting: I picked up the chair and tilted it at an angle, I cleaned the front legs and then tilted it the other way and cleaned its back, too. I was totally absorbed in what I was doing, when suddenly I felt the man breathing on my neck, giving off a stink of alcohol. He pressed against me from behind, put his arms around me in a tight grip and hissed, "Leave the chair and come to me. I won't hurt you. You are a beautiful girl, it's such a pity" — and then he suddenly burst out laughing. He bent his head and was about to kiss me. I pushed him away forcefully and slipped out of his clutches. Terribly upset and frightened, I still managed to say, "Excuse me, Sir, leave me alone. I am a little girl of fourteen. You must have a wife at home, so why do you need me?" The guard, stunned at my brazenness, backed off and looked at me, and then, as though pushed by some hidden hand, left the room.

I stood rooted to the spot for a few minutes, unable to move a muscle, in some sort of blackout, shaking all over. I couldn't believe that the man had just walked away without satisfying himself. I knew exactly what the guard wanted and had talked stuff and nonsense about his wife and his home. Could that possibly have been what deterred him?

When I got back to the basement, I tearfully related what

had happened. We discussed the guard's unexpected reaction and came up with the conjecture that maybe he had a daughter my age and for a split second had imagined her in my place. During the days that followed, I was afraid of meeting that guard again, or other guards, because the next time things might end differently. Later I heard that more than one Jewish woman had been raped in that building. I was very fortunate that Divine Providence prevented the man from doing the terrible deed.

Another day of nervous expectation passed. Father, always creative, conceived of another revolutionary idea, one that sounded foolhardy, perhaps even mad: to escape! After the war, we learned that of the thousands of people who were imprisoned in the building before us, not one had worked up the courage to even consider escaping.

That evening, when I returned from my work upstairs, Father asked me about the door handles on the offices. Could they be removed? The truth is that I had noticed that some of the handles were loose and once the handle of the door to the washroom, which was next to the offices, actually came off in my hand. Father tried to persuade me to remove one of the handles and bring it back to the basement. The best place to hide it, he said, was in my undergarments. To encourage me, Father said he was confident I would succeed and that with the help of the handle we would be able to escape.

Why did Father want a door handle? How could such a simple object help us get out of a well-guarded prison?

Then Father told us his bold plan. Christmas Eve, which would be in two days, was the best time to act. Most of the guards would be home celebrating with their families. Only a few guards would remain upstairs in the building and they would probably get drunk. None of them would even think of coming down to the basement, as they would be too busy stuffing themselves with food and guzzling alcohol. In the meantime, we would open the door to the coal cellar with my door handle, then climb the pile of coal and slip out through the narrow opening to the street.

Well, we all thought the idea was quite mad. To begin with, the opening was barely 30 centimeters wide and we would not be able to get through it. And even if we somehow managed to crawl out, the street would be filled with people—how could we suddenly appear on the sidewalk without being seen? Josef had told us—perhaps he heard it from people in Nitra before the last transport—that no one had ever succeeded in escaping from the building during the whole period of the deportations. It was a pipe dream, he said.

But Father thought that on Christmas Eve, the family holiday, when everyone was at home happily eating the traditional meal after attending the solemn church service, the streets would be completely empty. The first one out would signal that there was no one about and then run across the road and hide in the railroad car that stood right across from the opening. Once we were all out, we would load our things on our shoulders (including the quilt, which was worth more than its weight in gold) and walk slowly and normally, so as not to arouse suspicion. We would return to the village of Jarok, where the "safe" pit awaited us. The timing was good: The war was intensifying, Allied planes were bombing the city, houses were being destroyed and people were being killed. Many of the inhabitants were fleeing with their belongings to surrounding villages, which were safer. So there would be nothing suspicious or strange about a group of people walking out of the city and carrying parcels.

We continued to raise doubts and argue about the plan, but in the end we came round to Father's way of thinking and soon believed as firmly as he did that the escape would succeed. We felt dizzy at the very idea and intoxicated at the thought of being free. Naturally, we let Josef and the other family in on the secret; if they did not come with us, they were liable to be punished after we disappeared.

But there was still one big worry. Would I be able to take a door handle without anyone noticing? I was very afraid. I was especially afraid that the man who had tried to rape me would come back, place his hands on me, and feel the handle hidden in my clothes. But I said nothing, because I knew that if I raised such fears the plan would be abandoned in order to protect me.

Ronny understood my distress. He, too, had a difficult problem. That day, a container filled with coal had fallen on his foot while he was working in the coal cellar. Two of his toes had been crushed and were now bruised, swollen and extremely painful. Writhing with pain, he whispered to me, "Even if we do escape, how will I be able to walk all the way to the village when my foot hurts so much and is bleeding?"

I didn't know what to say to encourage him, the more so because all I could think about was my mission.

I hardly slept a wink that night. All I could think about was that as soon as I removed a door handle, one of the guards would notice that it was missing. Immediately they would suspect me and interrogate me mercilessly to find out why I had taken the handle. Would I have the strength to do the job? I'm sure I wasn't the only one who was tormented by these questions. All the others must have been thinking the same thing and having the same doubts. Finally I fell into a troubled sleep, broken by terrible nightmares that left me very frightened.

The morning of December 23 arrived. The guard who took me upstairs said that today I would be cleaning but the next day, Christmas Eve, I could stay with the others in the basement. He was friendlier than usual and even sat with us a bit to describe how he was going to spend the holiday with his family.

I went upstairs, as I did every morning. This office, where I had worked before, had only one door, leading to the corridor. I knew that today was my one and only chance to steal a door handle, which might save us and lead us to freedom. I pulled the handle but it didn't budge—it was held fast by a screw, I saw. What to do? Where could I find another handle? I started cleaning the office but I was so nervous that my hands wouldn't obey me.

Around noon, I went out into the corridor, off which there were offices. Most of them were empty, as were two washrooms. I stood absolutely still and listened for any noise. I heard chairs being dragged on the floor above me, which was the dining room. The guards must be having their lunch. Afterward the regular guard would bring me something to eat and might lock me in. I had to find a door handle right away. It was now or never!

I tiptoed down the corridor and tried all the handles. I opened door after door, tried to remove the handle, and then closed the door again. Finally I succeeded: one handle came off easily. I felt flushed and started to perspire all over. I replaced the outside handle and removed the inside one. I closed the door using the handle that remained and put the other handle under my arm, pressing it down. Then I tiptoed back, almost at a run, to the office I was supposed to be cleaning. I hid the handle among some papers on a shelf and went on with my work.

Soon a guard I didn't know arrived with food. I received a larger portion than usual, along with a special delicacy in honor of the holiday. I was terribly nervous but tried to behave naturally. Toward the end of the day, just before the guard appeared to escort me back down, I took the handle and again held it under my arm.

My heart raced when the guard showed up. He was the regular guard and he greeted me gaily, already entering into the holiday atmosphere, and said I should hurry because he had to rush home to decorate the tree and prepare the presents for his family. I tried to look calm but my hands shook and I felt hot all over. However, the guard noticed nothing. He made a superficial check to see that the office was clean and told me to follow him. I kept my arm pressed tightly against my side to keep the handle from slipping. I glanced at the guard fearfully, but he was relaxed and told me that today the prisoners too would get a more festive meal. In the basement, he parted from us with a holiday greeting, as though we were also celebrating, and rushed off.

As his footsteps faded, everyone looked at me expectantly. I took out the "treasure" and then collapsed onto the floor and released my tension in tears. Ronny came over and patted my head. Everyone looked at me gratefully and hugged and kissed me, but I was still terribly frightened that someone would notice the missing door handle. Naturally, the Jewish girl who cleaned the offices would be suspected first. But the evening passed peacefully. Father hid the handle in a safe place and we started to go over the details of the daring plan that would be carried out on Christmas Eve.

Christmas Eve

The atmosphere was different on the morning of December 24. There was plenty of hustle and bustle, sounds of singing and music from upstairs filled the prison. Still, a guard came as usual to open the door of the coal cellar with the handle he brought with and then took away.

In addition to a jug of tea and slices of bread—our normal breakfast—we received some baked goods to mark the holiday. Josef, the guards' favorite, also received cigarettes and sausage. The guard told the men to be especially quick in filling the coal containers today. They would have to finish by the early afternoon, he said, so he could lock the coal cellar before going home to celebrate the holiday with his family.

It was freezing cold outside, after a night of snow, and the burners had to be kept lit. So the men had to work despite the holiday atmosphere. Soon, only a few guards would be left in the building, and the city would come to a standstill by the middle of the afternoon. Even public transportation would stop until the next morning. I remembered Christmas Eve from when I was a little girl in Michalovce, when the streets were decorated and lit up and colorful

Christmas trees in the squares gave everything a festive look. I remember being especially struck by the contrast between the shiny white snow and the dark green of the trees. But tonight everything would be dark—the street lights would not be turned on, there would be no decorations or trees in public places, and colorful lights would not shine from windows—because the war still raged and the bombs fell without taking account of holidays. This was our opportunity. After dark, we would carry out our fateful plan.

The time crept by with agonizing slowness. The day seemed longer than ever to me. Because I didn't have to work, I went to the coal cellar to watch the men work—Father, the three boys and Mr. Simon. They were working energetically in order to load the amount of coal needed. I watched their rhythmic movements as they scooped up the lumps of coal with their wide shovels, heaved them into a container and then repeated the process again and again. Ronny gritted his teeth as he worked: he was in agony because of the pain in his foot, but he insisted on working, so the others would not have to do more.

I glanced at the narrow opening through which we would have to crawl. It didn't seem possible. Maybe the children would make it through, but what about the adults? True, they were thin after eating so little and so poorly for many months, but they were still wider than us children. And even if we did succeed, what awaited us on the outside, and especially on the way? How long, and in what conditions could we keep running and hiding in order to survive? What would happen when we suddenly appeared on the street?

Anyone who happened by, any drunk, could turn us in. I was seized by a terrible unease. I tried to cast out the doubts and worries, but they kept coming back and gnawed at my heart. This time, I thought, Father hadn't taken into account the fact that even if we succeeded in getting away, the escape of a group of people, including children, from a prison would be a terrible insult to the armed guards who were in charge of us, and they would therefore try doubly hard to catch and punish us—not only for the escape, but because of their shame and our effrontery.

The sun inclined toward the west. In another moment the guard would come to lock the coal cellar and bring us our tea and bread, as he did every evening. We waited for him, totally on edge. We collected our few clothes in a corner together with the quilt, which we tied with the rope we had found. Time seemed to pass in unbearably slow increments.

We tensed up as we heard the guard approaching: Would he notice anything different about our behavior? No—he was in a hurry: He put the food down, locked the coal cellar, put the handle into his pocket and left at once. When we could no longer hear his footsteps, we went over the plan one last time. Soon we would open the door to the coal cellar with the handle I had taken. One of us would stand guard by the stairs to warn the others if he heard anyone coming. We decided on the order for leaving. The four members of the Simon family would go first, then us, and finally Josef and the three boys.

Evening fell. Zero hour. Father inserted the metal handle into the slot of the coal cellar door, turned it—and the door opened. There was a full moon outside, which illuminated the pile of coal. All was silent and tranquil, except for the pounding of our hearts. The Simon family said goodbye to us with hugs and kisses, and with quavering voices we wished them luck: they had chosen a different escape route and would not be joining us. They entered the coal cellar and each of them climbed to the top of the pile, leaving their clothes covered in soot. With an effort, Mr. Simon managed to crawl through the narrow opening and waited on the sidewalk. Then came his two children, their mother pushing them one after the other into their father's waiting arms. A minute later, she too disappeared through the opening. The Simon family was suddenly gone.

Just as our turn to leave came, we got a signal to return immediately. The lookout heard someone approaching. We froze. Panic seized us. We were lost, this was the end! Father closed the coal cellar door and removed the handle. We sat down on our straw mattresses, as though getting ready for sleep, first scattering some clothes on the Simons' empty mattresses along with the quilt. Gloomily, we waited for events to take their course. The guard would surely see that four people were missing and we would be sent immediately to the coordination point and then to the East.

A young man of about 20 wearing a Hlinka Guard uniform appeared at the bottom of the stairs. Smiling affably, he went over to Josef, his old buddy, and offered him a cigarette. He said he was bored and lonely on this Christmas Eve—his friends were with their families and he was left almost alone on guard duty. His breath smelled of alcohol, his eyelids were heavy and the pupils seemed to roll about strangely. He must have been drunk. Every once in a while he looked around, went on talking and laughing, and said he was happy that tonight there would be no air raids, thanks to the holiday. Laying himself down on a mattress, he stayed until it became quite late, while we prayed silently that he wouldn't ask about the missing prisoners. Possibly he didn't even know that there were new prisoners, so he would not notice their absence. Finally, he got up, stretched, and wished us good night and a happy holiday. He went up the stairs and disappeared. Again we had been saved from disaster! "The grace of heaven is upon us," Father whispered.

As soon as he was gone, we rushed almost hysterically to get on with our escape. We dressed quickly and re-tied the quilt. Father opened the door again and climbed to the top of the coal pile. He reminded us that as soon as we were outside we were to run across the road, enter the railroad car across the way and wait for the others.

Mother was the first out—she had no difficulty because she was so thin—and we three girls followed one after the other. The brutal cold struck us like a slap on the face. I rushed to the railroad car with mother and my sisters, and we climbed in and kept our eyes peeled on the basement opening. We saw Father crawl out and then wait for the boys to push the quilt through as he pulled from his end. But the quilt was apparently stuck; he couldn't get it out. So as not to tear the cloth and release all the feathers, Father pushed the quilt back into the basement. Again and again they tried, always with the same result, and despite everything, we couldn't help laughing because it was truly funny. Then Father signaled to the boys inside and the quilt was pulled back in and disappeared from view. Suddenly, Father took a few steps and bent down as though tying a shoelace. We saw a group of people approaching, laughing loudly, in good spirits. They were shoving one another playfully, having a good time and probably drunk. They had obviously startled Father, which was why he moved away from the opening. But they passed him by without even a glance.

That surrealistic scene of Father pulling the quilt through the opening of the coal cellar in the basement of the central prison on Christmas Eve, in the heart of the city and in semi-darkness, is etched sharply in our memories. All it takes is a certain word or movement, or the touch of a down quilt, to instantly conjure up the sight.

After the revelers had passed, Father returned to the opening and signaled the boys to push the quilt out again. Again it got stuck, but we knew that Father would not give up. In this bitter cold, the quilt was our best hope of not freezing to death. That's why Father was so stubborn about getting it out. And finally he did it. The quilt was in his hands, he put it on his shoulder and rushed over to join us. Then Josef and two of the boys appeared one after the other and ran across the road.

We were all in the railroad car, except for Eli, Ronny's brother. We waited and waited but he didn't appear. What could be keeping him? We listened hard and strained to see in case he was calling out to us or signaling to us in some way, but we heard and saw nothing. Maybe he had been caught. Our nerves were already strained without this new tension. Josef lost his patience and decided to leave. He said he would go to the home of someone he knew, who would hide him. We parted from him emotionally. Although we had known him only for a short time, the shared destiny that was forced on us had made us very close and we were as concerned for him as we would be for a close relative.

After waiting a long time for Eli, we decided, with much agonizing, that there was no choice but to go on without him. Any further delay would mean that we would not be able to reach Jarok while it was still dark and get safely to the wine cellars — the only place that could serve as a shelter for the period ahead. I saw the disappointment and grief in Ronny's eyes. He hesitated about whether to go with us and leave his brother to an unknown fate, or to wait for him. Finally he was persuaded that there was nothing he could do to save him and he joined us.

On the street, Father carried the rolled quilt, while my little sister, Miriam, rode on the shoulders of Yaki, the older boy, and the rest of us each carried a parcel of clothes. The streets were empty, both because it was so late and because of the Christmas holiday. After a while we met a group of people; they looked at us in amazement but only wished us a happy holiday. We returned the greeting and added, without being asked, that we were on our way to relatives in a village, where we would spend the holiday and escape the air raids. It sounded logical enough. As I mentioned before, many of the city's inhabitants went to nearby villages, some in horse-drawn carts, others on foot. The exodus usually took place at night, when there were fewer air raids.

The cold froze our hands and feet. Fortunately we had

warm head coverings and winter clothes, which we had taken from the apartment, along with the quilt. We walked fast in order to warm ourselves, especially our feet, and to reach the village before dawn. There was still a long way to go. Ronny, who had a hard time walking, lagged behind. I stayed by his side. He was in agony—in physical agony because of his foot and in mental agony because of concern for his brother, and his conscience tore at him for not having waited. He whispered to me faintly that if his brother did not turn up, he would return to the city in the morning and turn himself over to the authorities and thus be reunited with him. He thought that Eli must have been caught and sent back to the prison. Ronny and Eli were all that remained of the family, and if Eli was taken, Ronny would be left alone in the world. I tried to comfort him. I urged him to continue to believe that they would soon be reunited. After all, we had hardly met anyone on the way, because they were all celebrating: They were not thinking about the Jews and it was far from certain that Eli had been caught. There was still a good chance that he would find his way to "our" pit. I think Ronny was heartened by my words, and we pushed on, occasionally looking back to make sure we were not being followed.

We could only imagine the guards' reaction in the morning when they found the prison empty. They would undoubtedly go wild with rage and accuse one another, but, above all, they would not be able to figure out how we had opened the coal cellar, which was the only place where there was an opening to the outside. Certainly they would feel humiliated, since none of the thousands of Jews who had been imprisoned there during the war had escaped before. Yet, now, a group that included children and had no means of any sort had daringly and skillfully outwitted the guards and escaped from a supposedly secure prison.

We were sure that we would be the target of an extensive search in order to bring us back and deport us. Would we reach our destination before they tracked us down? Fortunately, they had no way of knowing where we were headed, because the village of Cabaj-Čápor, where we had found shelter with the peasant who betrayed us, lay in the opposite direction from Jarok, where we had hidden beneath the ground.

The night was clear, but very cold. The stars glittered and a bright moon lit our way. After many hours of walking, we finally saw the first silos, in which we had hidden when we first came to the village. Our goal was to get to the cellars, which lay between these structures and the outlying houses.

We still remembered the way to the pit where we had hidden until three and a half weeks before. We restrained ourselves from shouting with joy when we reached the pit and simply crawled into it without further ado. Father closed the opening, just as he used to. We were happy, still not fully believing that we had carried out such a daring plan so successfully and had even found "our" pit. Father said jokingly that all we needed now was a *minyan*—ten males over the age of 13—so we could say the thanksgiving prayer. Only Ronny could not share in the general happiness. He was still depressed because of his brother and said he would wait only until the morning. If Eli didn't show up by then, he said, he would return to the prison to find him. We tried to cheer him up and talk him out of giving himself up, because we knew that the authorities would torture him until he revealed our hiding place.

We organized for the night in total silence and then covered ourselves with the soft quilt and fell asleep instantly. Before lying down, I tried to comfort Ronny again, but he wouldn't speak or come close to me. He remained silent and aloof, immersed in his grief. I wanted so much to make things easier for him, to lie next to him, but he was closed and remote.

A short time later, before the sun rose, we heard noises above and then someone started to move the boards and the straw from the opening. We froze in horror. Had our persecutors found our footsteps and followed us all the way here? A shadowy figure crawled toward us and a moment later we heard Eli's familiar voice.

As soon as he identified himself, Eli broke down in tears. The two brothers fell into each other's arms and then we all embraced him and bombarded him with questions. He told us that as he was about to make his escape, he heard footsteps and saw a passing figure that frightened him. He ran to the far end of the train, hid in the last car, and remained there for a long time, for fear he would be discovered. When he finally dared to come out, he looked for us in the car we had all run to, but we had already left. Eli understood that we had not been able to wait any longer. By the time he set out, we were far ahead. He also decided to take a roundabout route and stopped to hide every once in a while, and that was why it took him so long to arrive.

There are no words to describe our joy at being together again. Our hearts overflowed and we gave thanks for our great fortune. With uplifted spirits, we recalled how we had experienced one miracle after another in the past few months. We lay down again, utterly spent, and let Eli warm himself under the quilt. Before we drifted off, Father was already wondering how we would get word to Vincent that we were back, so that with his help we could again get the food that the good-hearted villagers collected for us.

"Grandmother, you didn't tell me what happened to the Simon family, who escaped from the prison first. Did you ever see them again, or Josef the shoemaker?" Omer asked.

"After the war, we learned, to our great sorrow, that they had not been as lucky as us. A few days after the escape, the Simon family was caught and they were all sent to a concentration camp. The mother and the two children perished, but the father survived—alone, ill and despairing. We met him after the war, but we could hardly recognize him. We saw an old, thin man who was very bitter and could barely hide his envy that we had survived. Josef's fate was also bitter. The day after the escape, while he was still on the run, gardists tracked him down and called to him to stop, and when he didn't, they shot and killed him. We were very sorry to hear the news about Josef's tragic end. We mourned for him for days."

Pneumonia

After our dramatic escape from prison we felt as though we were in a dream. Reality was more amazing than anything we could imagine. When we woke up after the longest night of our lives, we told the unbelievable story over and over. Now, though, we would have to return to the old routine. First we had to contact the Tokoly family and ask them to provide us with food again. I can't remember how we dared inform Vincent in broad daylight that we were back. But I remember well that on that very day, Christmas Day 1944, our savior couple arrived with food. The kisses and embraces and the wiping away of tears are all vividly engraved in my memory. Over and over, they asked us to tell the incredible story from the moment we were captured at the home of the peasant from the neighboring village to our escape from prison. They cried out in astonishment and in their eyes I could see how much they admired us for our daring. They even called us heroes. Word soon spread through the village about the Jewish family that had not given up and had dared to escape with their children from the best-guarded prison in the district. The villagers now seemed more willing than ever to help us. They saw our escape as a heroic act and as a miracle that was a divine sign.

After a day or two, when it became clear that the authorities were not searching for us, life in the pit resumed its boring routine of days that seemed to go on forever. On Sundays, Vincent brought food, as he had before. The old year ended, and on New Year's Day 1945, the Tokoly brothers surprised us by arriving in the middle of the day, bearing food, drinks and baked goods to celebrate. The village priest was again generous, sending a large quantity of preserved meat, sausages and apples.

During the first three days of the new year, the brothers visited us often. They brought us food and showered us with caring. Vincent sat with us for hours and we exchanged small talk by the light of the kerosene lamp. The rumors about the approaching end of the war naturally made us happy. The Germans were being defeated on every front, we were told, and the underground was becoming stronger. The Soviet Army had already liberated much of eastern Slovakia from the lengthy occupation. We were swept up by Vincent's enthusiasm and started to believe that salvation was at hand.

But despite the hopes, our friend also cautioned us not to leave the pit in daylight. The danger had not passed. In fact, the Germans, frustrated by their defeats in battle, were desperately attempting to exact revenge by hunting down the remaining Jews and those who assisted them. They were brutal to Jews whom they found in hiding, sometimes not bothering to organize a transport, but executing them on the spot. That is what happened in Banska Bystrica, for example. The Jews there were liberated by the partisans, but then the Germans counter-attacked and recaptured the city. They then hanged all the Jews, including my friend Yehudit, as I have already mentioned.

In addition to all their other gifts, Vincent and Anna let us wash at their house. They knew how badly we suffered from the impossible hygienic conditions and that it was impossible to bathe in the ice-cold water of the spring. They invited us to their house at night for a hot bath followed by a rest and a light meal.

Everything was ready when we entered their modest, warm home. A large round tub filled with steaming hot water stood in one corner of the room. My sisters and I were the first to remove our filthy clothes and get into the tub. It had been ages since we experienced the pleasure of hot water running over our bodies. We held our breath and plunged under the water, and then Mother washed our hair. What a delight it was when the water cascaded down from our hair to our shoulders! Washing away the outer dirt also seemed to relieve the inner pressures. I felt a pleasurable lightness. After us, Mother and Father took turns washing, using the same water. There was also talk of sending our clothes to be washed.

Returning to the pit, we felt wonderful, filled with renewed optimism that the end of the war was at hand. In the meantime, though, the fighting continued and we had to stay in hiding.

On the day after our visit to the Tokolys, I woke up in the middle of the night, shaking all over. My head felt terribly heavy, I felt nauseous, and my whole body felt strange. I coughed so loudly that some of the others woke up. I told Mother that my throat and head hurt, and I shook so badly that my teeth rattled, even though the warm quilt covered me up to my chin.

Mother put her hand on my forehead and said I had a raging fever and that my condition was serious. I must have caught a chill in the cold after the warm bath, she said anxiously. She roused Father and they tried to decide what to do. How could they deal with this problem? Amazingly, despite all we had been through, none of us had fallen ill until now. Not even a cold, still less a bad cough or flu. This was a new worry. No one knew exactly what was wrong with me, and of course there were no medicines—it was impossible even to make a cup of hot tea in the conditions of the pit.

The whole next day I lay under the quilt, shaking badly and burning up with a high fever, and every once in a while attacked by a lengthy coughing fit. The stale, heavy air in the pit certainly did me no good, but going out into the cold and danger was out of the question. The only "treatment" available was a piece of cloth dipped in snow placed on my forehead to cool me down and lower my temperature.

On Sunday, after I hadn't eaten anything for two days and had only wet my lips occasionally with a bit of water, the Tokolys arrived with the weekly provisions. Seeing me covered from head to foot with the quilt, and hearing that I had been feverish for three days, they said there was an epidemic of infectious pneumonia in the village. Many people had fallen ill, especially children. Some had been hospitalized in the city and a two-year-old boy had died.

Suddenly Anna said something that was so typical of these simple, direct, unsophisticated village folk. Clasping her hands together, she exclaimed: "Oh, what will we do if Aliska dies? Where will we bury her? We have only a Christian cemetery in the village and we won't be able to lay her to rest there, for sure!"

That was her main concern. She didn't suggest medicines — which apparently were not available in the village in any case — or help of any other kind. She accepted the illness as a decree from heaven. Everything was determined in advance; whatever happened was destined to happen. Life's passages flowed naturally in the village and each stage of existence — birth, maturity, reproduction, old age, illness, death — was accepted unquestioningly as part of the natural cycle.

Fortunately, Mother didn't understand what Anna said, or she would have been very frightened. The high fever also caused fainting spells and sometimes I blacked out. Everyone was terribly anxious about me. And what would happen if the others also caught the disease? I'm sure they must have worried that I might die here, in the pit, if I didn't get medical help. So desperate were Mother and Father that they even considered taking me to a doctor in the village, even if this meant being caught and deported. They asked me what I thought of the idea, but I said I was completely against it and promised to get better.

We were encouraged by the pounding of the Allies' artillery, as the front came ever closer to the village: Every day the noise of the battle became clearer and sharper. As soon as the Soviet troops reached the village, we would be rescued and know freedom again. If only it would happen quickly, so my illness could be treated. I was not yet better. Most of the time, I slept deeply. I hardly ate. Fortunately, I drank a lot of water, and that was probably what kept me alive. My body grew very weak. I hardly got up. This period, too, has disappeared completely from my memory, and it was only thanks to others that I know what happened to me.

One day in that cold January of 1945, Father returned from emptying out the pail of excrement, which he did every morning, to say that the sun was shining, the sky was perfectly clear, and that even though it was cold, the air was pure and fresh. He made a tempting offer, which I was more than ready to accept. If I agreed, he said, he would take me outside for a bit, for some fresh air. Everyone thought it was a good idea. When I asked him how cold it was, he said I could wrap myself in everyone's warm clothes and even in the quilt. I longed for a little daylight and air. I hadn't been outside since that visit to the village at the beginning of the month and I longed to feel the sun's warm rays on my face.

Mother helped me put on a few layers of clothing and she covered my head with a kerchief. With Father and Ronny helping me, I managed to climb out of the pit. After days of lying down, I could barely stand on my feet and I leaned on the two of them. The sun and snow dazzled me and I kept opening and shutting my eyes. But I couldn't bear the light of day and I could see nothing—only a shining white that hurt my eyes. I asked Father and Ronny whether they could see anything. They also found it difficult to get used to the sudden sharp light, but their eyes soon adjusted and they described to me what they saw: bare trees whose branches looked as if they were about to snap under the heavy weight of snow, the silos and huts, and the open area between us and the village.

We stayed there for some time, but I still couldn't see anything. Then I thought with horror that maybe I would never be able to see again. Father and Ronny thought that my weakness from the high fever and not eating had affected my eyes, but that this was only temporary and would soon pass. But I was still very upset. I rubbed my eyes, I blinked, but I still couldn't see anything except shifting blotches of dark and light.

Suddenly I felt terribly nauseous. I would have fallen without the support of Father and Ronny. They walked me slowly around the pit. I said I wanted to rest and they helped me sit down on the snow-covered ground. Tears ran down my cheeks and my heart pounded. Had I lost my eyesight? I had a lengthy coughing fit and spat out the phlegm, staining the snow. Father and Ronny were appalled to see that the color was brownish red: Did that mean I was bleeding in the lungs? But I couldn't see the look of terror on their faces or the color of the phlegm (They told me about it later, after I got well). They decided to return me to the pit at once. They half-dragged me and I felt myself pulled along, with no strength at all.

Back in the pit, I heard the others whispering. But it was only later that I learned about the concern of my family and friends. They were arguing about whether they had the right to damage my health. The family had to decide what to do under these very trying circumstances, in which they were powerless to act or to find a reasonable solution. Should they take an example from battlefield, where a decision sometimes had to be made about whether to abandon a wounded soldier and save the others, or try to rescue him and risk losing everyone?

I coughed up more and more phlegm—the turning point in my illness came after I had got rid of most of the congestion in my lungs. Finally my fever began to abate. I started eating a little and my strength slowly returned. Every once in a while, I went out to breathe some fresh air. Still, I was panicky because my eyesight hadn't yet returned to normal, and I was afraid of going blind. The coughing, though, had almost gone away. As I grew stronger, I was able to take part in conversations and storytelling again, to the delight of everyone. I became as alert as ever and miraculously recovered. My full sight returned, too. And it all happened despite the intolerable conditions and even though we had no medicines.

(After the liberation, I was examined in a lung clinic. The doctors found a dark layer, a kind of wrapping around the lung covering. I was sent for a lengthy convalescence to the Tatra Mountains, and there, in the high air, in a pine forest, I was finally cured of the infectious phlegm that I had developed from inhaling the moisture in the pit for months.)

In February, the coldest month of the year, we were forced to stay in the pit even during the evening, when we liked to steal outside for some fresh air. The days were short but seemed very long, and unpleasant friction and arguments sometimes developed in our small group. Living in such close quarters without any privacy caused tension and quarrels—amazingly, there was never a real blow-up.

Ronny and I were the only ones who weren't bored. We found opportunities for mutual exploration and passed the long, dreary hours with confessions of love and dreams for the future. At twilight, when it was our turn to go to the spring and bring water, we were happy to be alone. We walked hand in hand, and despite the cold we put off our return to the pit as long as we could. Those were our only romantic "outings" and had to serve as a substitute for the hikes and other experiences of ordinary young people in normal times. Every day that passed infused us with new hope for a better future.

When March failed to bring the liberation we all craved, we began to doubt whether the end was really as close as we had hoped and believed. We had been denizens of the depths for almost half a year now, apart from three weeks in prison and the days we hid at Cabaj-Čápor until we were betrayed. The dark, dank pit made us depressed and we felt as though we were degenerating and losing our spirit. We impatiently awaited reports that the front was approaching, but the sounds of battle we heard actually seemed to be growing fainter. Our fears were reinforced when Vincent told us that there had been a temporary setback in the advance of the Allied forces and that the Germans seemed to be recovering and fighting back. They were massing their remaining troops for one last effort and sacrificing their youth on the altar of their pride. We were shocked to hear that boys of 16 and even younger had been thrown into battle. But despite tens of thousands of casualties, the

Germans were continuing their pointless war, Vincent said.

We now allowed ourselves to venture out more frequently. Two of us went up, in turn, for about a quarter of an hour at a time. I liked to listen to the sounds of the shelling and watch the flashes of exploding bombs. During this period we were again invited to the home of Vincent and Anna to bathe. The old rules of caution were cast aside, as the Germans and their henchmen no longer tried to capture Jews.

March was about to end, and according to Father's calculations it would soon be time to celebrate Passover, the Festival of Freedom. For many hours he regaled us with the story of how our people was enslaved in Egypt and about Moses and the miracles that befell the Jews in those days. He talked about the symbolism of this time in our lives: We too were eager to be delivered from slavery into redemption and from darkness to light.

One day toward the end of the month, we suddenly felt a powerful jolt. The earth shook all around us. That morning, Vincent had come to tell us with great excitement that the Russians were approaching and that the villagers were frightened in the face of the unknown future. There were rumors that those who had collaborated with the Nazis in the city of Nitra, the district town where we had been imprisoned, were in a panic. They were said to be running around like mice with no way out of their hole and no place to escape to. The informers and betrayers were trying to erase their past, fearing revenge. The partisans were attacking everywhere, derailing German supply trains and staying hard on the heels of the enemy. Many members of the Hlinka Guard were defecting and trying to deny their activity in the force, but those who were caught by the partisans were executed. Many of the districts in eastern Slovakia were already liberated and the few Jews who remained there in hiding or had passed themselves off as gentiles had been freed and were now protected. The reports fired us with hope. We began to grasp that our own harsh and prolonged period in hiding might be over within days.

The Russians Arrive

Winter passed. The air became fragrant with the approaching spring. The chirping of the birds returning from their migration filtered down into the depths of the earth and stimulated our dormant, indifferent senses. Toward evening, when we allowed ourselves to go outside for some fresh air, we avidly breathed in the intoxicating scent of the new growth. The hope in our hearts also took on new life, in the belief that we would soon be liberated.

One morning in the beginning of April, as Mother was handing out the portions of bread with a slice of hard white cheese, which was our breakfast, the ground beneath us shook. The sand walls seemed about to cave in and clods of earth rained down on us from above. We looked up at the roof of the pit; it had no support and we were afraid it would collapse on us. The kerosene lamp, which hung on one of the walls of the pit, and which we had lit for the meal, shook and fell off its hook—but someone caught it in the air and it didn't crash onto the ground and break.

As in a movie when the film tears and the characters on the screen are transfixed in mid-action, we all froze and looked at one another in terror. Nearly everyone dropped their piece of bread because our hands were shaking with fright. Was it an earthquake, which would bury us in this dark hole forever? And why now, after our years of suffering and flight, when liberation was just around the corner? Our immediate thought was to get out as fast as possible, despite the risk of being discovered. While we were still hesitating, there was another tremendous jolt, even stronger than the one before. Father quickly put out the lamp and told us to be silent and wait to see what developed.

One of the boys whispered that what we were hearing and feeling came from artillery shelling, aerial bombing or grenades exploding very close by. He volunteered to go up top and see what was going on, and before anyone could say anything, he was already making his way out. But before he reached the top, the earth trembled again. There was a huge explosion, the ground shook, and the boy slid down, either because of the force of the blast or out of sheer fright. Gasping, he said he had seen only flashes of light, which were followed immediately by the explosions. A battle must be raging right above us, he said. We began to grasp the scale of the event, which for us meant a true turning point. But what were we to do? Stay below and risk being buried alive, or go above ground and possibly be hit by bullets or shrapnel? And who could guarantee that outside we would encounter our liberators and not the retreating Germans, who would not hesitate to finish us off on the spot? We decided that for the time being we should stay in our shelter.

The bombardment resumed every few minutes, with

regular breaks. I found something to do that reduced my anxiety a little. I started to count the number of "booms" between one explosion and the next, and almost always arrived at the same number. So I could guess when the next explosion would come and prepare myself for it. Little by little, we got used to the noise, even though it was extremely frightening each time. Still, despite our fear, we felt happy and relieved, because we knew our fortunes were about to change.

The heavy bombardment went on for hours and then stopped as abruptly as it had begun. I counted to almost a thousand and still there was quiet. We kept expecting more explosions but the silence continued, unbroken. After the massive explosions, from which our ears were still ringing, the quiet seemed unreal. Were we really close to the end of the accursed war and the years of persecution, hiding, escape, anguish and hunger? Then, suddenly, we heard noises from above that grew constantly louder.

We tried to figure out what the cacophony might be. We heard muffled speech, shouts, groans, someone blowing a whistle, the heavy footsteps of a person or an animal, sounds of running and of objects being dragged across the ground. Our nerves were taut. We looked up, searching for clues about what was going on outside the pit. My stomach heaved with terror—my usual reaction to tension, as I knew by now—but I felt that a vast change was coming. Now would come the final act in the drama, and we would learn whether our destiny was life or, heaven forbid, death!

All of a sudden, we were dazzled by a ray of light coming through the opening above. Someone had moved the camouflage. The beam of light began to move across the pit and in perfect silence illuminated our faces one after the other, as though someone was surveying those in the crowded pit and was stunned to discover, in the bowels of the earth, children and adults blinking as the light shone on them. A figure crawled down toward us and we recoiled in horror as we saw that while in one hand he held a flashlight, in the other was a submachine gun, pointed at us. The figure who had entered the pit wore a uniform of some sort. We pushed back against the wall. Another split second and the man would be among us.

The man approached Father and aimed his weapon at him. Mother jumped up, like a lioness bent on protecting her cubs from an enemy, turned to the soldier, and said to him in German, being convinced that he was a Nazi: "Please don't hurt us, we are only refugees who are hiding from the bombs."

Hearing German, the soldier became angry and let out a juicy curse in Russian. Then he said, "*Kto vy nemtsi?*" (Are you Germans?) and aimed his weapon at Mother.

Father, who knew some Russian from time he spent with Russian forces in the First World War, immediately leaped toward the soldier, grabbed his arm, greeted him in Russian, and said: "*My yevrei*" (We are Jews). He went on, in somewhat broken Russian, "We escaped from the German criminals and we are hiding here."

Thunderstruck, the soldier dropped his weapon, sat down with us and, to our amazement, began to cry softly.

Father lit the lamp and we saw a young man who looked no more than 16. His face was as smooth as a child's. He wiped his tear-filled eyes and muttered a few broken words, which only Father understood, but which seemed to express deep anger. Father translated what turned out to be a series of curses and expletives that the soldier had leveled at the Germans for causing the humiliating situation in which we found ourselves. He cursed them because a family with little girls was forced to live under the ground like wild animals.

Without a word, we hugged and kissed him, causing him deep embarrassment. Father continued to translate his remarks and the many questions he plied us with. He wanted to hear everything about us. He told us that the war was not yet over, but that the Russian Army had reached our region and was in hot pursuit of the Germans. Right above us, the front was moving rapidly toward the west. As we spoke the soldier took a meat sandwich from his pocket and urged us to partake of it.

Seeing this young Russian soldier who came down into the pit without fear or hesitation, I was reminded of the Germans who tried to find out if there was anyone below by shooting into the pit. Those shots had made us take refuge in the village, where we were betrayed by the very person who hid us. Whereas those Germans hadn't dared enter the pit for fear of encountering partisans, and preferred to fire from above and take no risks, "our" Russian soldier had come down fearlessly, even though he didn't know who or what he might encounter. We asked him how he had guessed that there were people in this particular pit, out of all the other pits scattered around the field. He told us that while advancing with his unit, he had felt warm vapors rising from the opening and guessed that there must be people below. It was his duty to clarify the situation and to ensure that the unit's progress was not halted.

After we got over our surprise, we became friendly with the soldier. He suggested that we accompany him outside to get some air and meet the rest of the soldiers in his unit. We hadn't yet taken in the miracle. It was difficult to believe that this moment had finally come. We agreed immediately and willingly followed him out. By the time we were all out, he had gathered a few of his comrades and was telling them our story in brief. They were astonished to learn that we had lived under the ground for so long. But before we could take advantage of Father's Russian and start a serious conversation, shooting began again and there were explosions very close by. The soldiers told us to go back down immediately, though not before emptying their kitbags and giving us all the food they had, despite our protests.

We scrambled back down and sat side by side on the straw-covered ground. Suddenly, we all tried to express what we felt in a confused, noisy outburst, laughing and crying at the same time. A little while later another soldier, a young officer, came down. He told us he was Jewish — and stunned us by speaking in Yiddish. We were delighted to meet a member of our people, and not least because now we would be able to converse directly, without an interpreter, as we all knew some Yiddish and a few of us spoke it fluently. The officer told us that when he heard about the Jewish family that was hiding in a pit, he wanted to meet us at once and hear our story.

He listened attentively. Even if he knew about the

persecution of the Jews and the deportations, the long years of the war kept Russian soldiers like him from thinking very much about the hardships of the world outside or the fate of the Jews. Most of the time, they were busy planning and carrying out combat missions. The officer was shocked by our life of stagnation and the subhuman conditions of our existence. His young face showed anger and sadness at our ordeal, and he was happy that it had fallen to him to be among the liberators and bring us the news that deliverance was at hand. He promised that our situation would now improve and that our life of fear was about to change.

That whole wonderful day passed in a state of delirium. Again and again, we peeked out from the opening, unable to believe that our suffering was at an end. Russian troops visited us day and night. Soldiers and officers came and went in an unending flow, usually in pairs because the place was so small. Everyone wanted to see us and speak with us, even if we could communicate only with our eyes and sign language. Those who could brought food to cheer us up. In the meantime, the fighting continued and the explosions shook the walls of the pit.

At night, when quiet fell, we emerged from the pit and sat by a bonfire with the soldiers, who covered us with blankets and showered us with love. We responded with gratitude and admiration. While they sang melancholy songs to the accompaniment of an accordion, one of the soldiers turned to Father and said, *"Davay vodka."* We thought the soldier was thirsty and wanted water, as in Slovakian *voda* means water. Ronny and I got up at once and rushed to the spring with a pail. But when we offered the soldier the water, we could see that he was disappointed and even offended. He looked at us with barely contained rage, and if it hadn't been for his comrades, he might have struck us. Finally he mumbled a common curse and looked very hurt, as though he was the butt of a practical joke.

At the time we didn't understand that he had said "vodka" and meant the alcoholic drink (it was the first time I ever heard the word)—and we brought him water! His friends explained the misunderstanding to him, and seeing our innocent, frightened faces, he picked up the pail, spilled out the water, stamped his foot on the ground, mumbled something to himself, smiled and left.

Back in the pit later that night, my sisters fell asleep at once, but the rest of us were too excited to sleep. We talked about the events of the day and asked the questions that bothered us: What would tomorrow bring? Would we be able to return to our old home? Whom would we meet there? What happened to our cousin Simon, who had come with us from Hungary? What happened to the large families of Mother and Father, with whom we had been out of touch for so long? Where had the storm driven them? What about our friends? We knew it would be a long time before we could resume a normal life. Each of us tried to guess what sort of world awaited us "out there" after we cast off the barren, stagnant life we had endured, and how we would fit in to society again.

We talked about how we had to catch up on so much information and knowledge, about going back to our studies and about settling in the Land of Israel. It went without saying that we would not stay in a country where the majority of the people not only had done nothing to resist and prevent the deportation of the Jews, whose roots lay centuries deep in the soil here, but had actually assisted and willingly collaborated with the Nazi conquerors. True, we were no longer under threat of persecution, deportation and extermination, but our fears and unanswered questions troubled us. At the same time, we did not stop praising our great fortune. We looked back in anger and pain at the road of torment and suffering on which our people had been forced to embark, but in our case, at least, there was also a certain satisfaction: We had survived, thanks to resourcefulness and great daring.

The joy of liberation was not complete, though, because of our anxiety about the rest of the family. The three boys also could not free themselves of deep concern about the fate of their families. It was a new experience for us to realize that we would soon know whether others had come through the ordeal; during our long months of hiding, all our energy had been devoted to finding immediate solutions with just one goal: *survival.*

We were most concerned about our aged grandparents. It was hard to believe that they could have endured the deportation to "work" (We had no idea that they had been murdered in gas chambers and their bodies reduced to ashes in crematoria). Mother, pessimistic by nature, was seized by a profound sadness and assailed by pangs of conscience; she cried softly most of the time, even though we didn't know for certain whether our grandparents had perished. Her heart told her that she would never see them again. Most of our family died in the Holocaust.

On the day after our liberation, we emerged from the pit unafraid. We met more soldiers, who had heard the story of the Jews that lived in the depths of the earth, and the same scenes of sympathy repeated themselves. In the meantime, the front advanced toward the village of Jarok, home of the Tokoly family, and the sounds of battle grew distant and muffled.

We were permitted to venture into the area that was already liberated. The ground was pockmarked from the shelling, and we collected fragments from the bombs and cartridge cases. We also saw shocking sights, like the carcasses of horses with their eyes glazed over, petrified organs pointing skyward. A heavy, sickening smell hung over everything. Groans of wounded men being treated by medics could be heard from a large tent that served as a field clinic. When we approached a few covered trucks near the tent, we were told to back away: The trucks held the bodies of those killed in battle. As soon as the fighting slackened, they would be buried in temporary graves in the village. Shaken by a primal fear of death, I averted my gaze from the trucks and kept my distance.

Another day passed, and on the third day of our liberation, Father, his eyes aglow, told us that it was now the Hebrew month of Nissan and that soon we would celebrate Passover, the Festival of Freedom. Yet another miracle had befallen us: We ourselves were also being liberated and going from slavery to redemption. And God willing, Father said, we would celebrate the Seder night in Nitra, the city where we had been imprisoned and from which we had escaped. We hoped to get *matza* there and hold a proper Seder.

Father's words sounded like a wild fantasy. Who still remembered that there were holidays in the world, or knew when they fell? But Father had kept a careful count of the days, weeks and months. He observed the rise of the new moon every month and he knew the dates and times of the holy days. At Purim, too, he had waited for a miracle—the defeat of Hitler (the modern-day Haman of the Purim story who tried to destroy the Jewish people)—but when it did not come to pass, he refrained from telling us about his calculations.

Father had devised many plans so far, and we had accepted most of them with grave doubts. The hopes he expressed about our liberation and about holding the Seder sounded like yet another dream. But after thinking about it, we all had to admit that Father's many plans, which had seemed totally improbable, had eventually been carried out. Gradually we came to believe that whatever Father predicted stood a good chance of coming true.

From Darkness to Light

When we emerged from the pit the next morning, we learned that Jarok had been captured and was under curfew. We were glad of this, as it meant the end of our "Stone Age." Our period of running and hiding was over, and we would soon return to civilization and to a normal life. We asked one of the friendly officers whether we could at last leave the damp, odorous pit. We explained to him that one of the peasant families had helped us during our time of hardship and that we wanted to go to their house. The officer gave his approval, but advised us to wait until the end of the day before setting out, for fear we might be hit by stray bullets.

Toward evening we organized, gathered our few possessions—including the kerosene lamp and the famous quilt—took our leave of the soldiers and set off, escorted by two armed guards provided by the officer. For the last time, we looked back at the pit that had given us a safe haven for so long, and we felt deep gratitude. Now we were experiencing a metamorphosis: from hunted animals to human beings.

It was twilight by the time we reached the village. In the

gathering dusk we could make out a few figures walking about — they were soldiers, as the villagers were still forbidden to leave their homes. But there was a holiday atmosphere: No one had gone to work. We hurried to the home of the Tokolys. The gate was open and we entered the courtyard and knocked on the door. They had already seen us through the window and opened the door wide. We fell on them with kisses and embraces, all of us weeping in a mixture of sadness and joy. The soldiers who had escorted us wished us well and left. The three boys went on to the home of Pavel, their benefactor.

After the initial excitement wore off a little, we asked Vincent and Anna if we could bathe and remove the layers of dirt that had accumulated on our bodies. Naturally, we wanted to wash before going to sleep in their home. They made the preparations and also surprised us by quickly preparing a festive meal with everything they could scrape up. Their only daughter, Ela, who was Miriam's age, was delighted that they would be able to sleep in the same bed. The sumptuous meal around a table that was properly set, with us sitting on chairs — after having sat on the ground when eating during the months in the pit — and the marvelous hot, homemade food, such as we had rarely tasted for longer than we could remember, was a celebration in itself and rounded off the emotional encounter. We sat and talked with the couple for hours, and we thanked God, and also our hosts for being part of our deliverance.

We arranged to stay with them until Nitra was liberated. Once we returned to the apartment where we had lived until September 7, 1944, we would get in touch with them and return to visit. We wanted very much to repay them for their kindness and generosity. They would remain forever engraved in our hearts as symbols of humanity and of sheer goodness, of unconditional giving with nothing asked in return. We also looked forward to the first opportunity to express our deep gratitude to the noble priest in the village for his material and spiritual assistance.

The curfew was lifted the next day and the villagers were permitted to leave their homes. The streets quickly filled up with people. Children ran about wildly after days of being cooped up. Everyone made for the village square, by the church, where they milled about in small groups, talking and arguing, trying to figure out what the future held in store. We too wondered what sort of world would rise from the ruins; one thing we knew was that everything was going to change; nothing would be the same.

The priest emerged from the church and was immediately surrounded by the villagers, who waited their turn to kiss his hand in love. It was the first time we had seen him, and to me it seemed that an inner beauty radiated from him and that his tall, impressive figure reflected the soul within. We joined the line and when our turn came we introduced ourselves. The priest embraced Father and called him by his name, Moritz. His eyes grew moist as he shook hands with us. We expressed our profound thanks for his help, and he replied that he was grateful to us for affording him the great privilege of being able to assist us, although he felt he had not done enough. The believers were amazed at the warmth shown by the holy man toward Jews. The priest placed his hands together and blessed us. In his name and in the name of his congregation, he asked forgiveness and pardon from all the Jews who had suffered and perished, in no small measure because of the indifference of the non-Jewish population.

We watched the victory celebrations, which were held in cooperation with the liberating forces. During the celebrations, we ran into the three boys with whom we had shared the many months of hiding. Ronny and I tried to draw near and touch each other, but unlike the time in the pit, when the darkness hid us from the others, here, in broad daylight, we turned shy and became children again. Only our eyes expressed our love and our happiness at meeting again. Among the festive crowd, we met two more Jewish families who had been hidden by villagers. They were luckier than us, because they'd had a comfortable, safe home as their haven and did not have to hide in a moldy pit. The difference was that they had plenty of money and were able to pay for the mercy shown them by the villagers, who turned out to be decent folk and did not turn them in.

Everyone praised our courage and the resourcefulness and persistence we had shown in conditions fit only for animals. Most of them had already heard about our miraculous escape from the prison, which gave us an added aura of heroism in the eyes of the village folk.

During the next few days, we looked for ways to occupy ourselves. In the Tokolys' courtyard there was a well with a round opening made of red bricks, from which they drew their water. We amused ourselves by pulling up water in the pail that hung on the side of the well and then spilling it back. We climbed the huge tree that grew on the street and we visited the animals, feeding the two cows, the four pigs, the rabbits in the cages, and the chickens and ducks that wandered about freely in the courtyard and outside, too. The soldiers who befriended us when they found us in the pit came to visit. The Jewish officer promised that the new political situation would bring prosperity and well-being to everyone, and we believed him wholeheartedly. The first blossoms of spring added beauty and a feeling of hope.

One sunny, bright day, we were sitting in the yard and warming ourselves, when the officer we knew arrived. He asked for a drink of the clear, refreshing water we had just pulled up from the well, and I was happy to oblige him. However, before I could fill the glass, Vincent grabbed it from me in order to honor the guest with cool homemade wine. The glass broke in my hand and cut me deeply. Horrified, I saw that two fingers, the little finger and the ring finger, were hanging by a thread. We were all terribly frightened, especially Vincent, who felt that he was to blame and looked sad and embarrassed, on the brink of tears.

The officer rushed me to the tent clinic, which was now in the village. However, the doctor said that the cut was too deep and there was unfortunately no way to repair the nerves and veins. And he didn't have any painkillers or anesthetics. The pain was unbearable, I couldn't stop crying, the wound filled with pus and my hand hurt day and night. The result was that I lost the feeling at the ends of those two fingers. To this day, they are very sensitive, especially when it's cold, a painful souvenir that cast something of a pall over those heady days of liberation.

When the three boys heard what had happened, they came to visit in order to cheer me up.

In Nitra I was examined by a specialist, who said there was nothing to be done, as the nerves had been severed and had not been restored properly, which was the reason for the absence of feeling. Still, I thank God that this is my only disability from that time. Even now, more than 55 years later, the cut is still visible and I can't bend the injured fingers. They have remained stiff ever since, because of unprofessional treatment in wartime field conditions.

By the time we returned to Nitra and the small apartment we had abandoned before the "flood," most of Slovakia had already been captured by the Soviet army. A slow trickle of psychically and physically battered Jews, survivors of the concentration camps and the death camps, began to return to the city in the hope of finding their loved ones. The atmosphere was oppressive. Those who returned were broken in spirit and walked about the streets bent and frightened, constantly looking to all sides, deeply insecure. Many of them were *musselmen*—the name given to the former inmates of the camps, who looked like walking skeletons after years of malnutrition—and the sight of them shocked everyone.

After our return, we were able to rent a larger, more spacious apartment, and when the day of the first Seder arrived, we were privileged to celebrate the most meaningful holiday in our lives in a more comfortable house, just as Father had foreseen. We invited a few refugees who had lost their whole families. They were sad-eyed and found it difficult to rejoice with us. For us, the holiday was a very significant event that symbolized our liberation, too. Ever since, whenever we gathered for the Seder and the reading of the Hagadah and came to the line "When Israel came forth from Egypt," Father would add, "And when we came forth from Jarok, we were as dreamers..."

From that first Passover of our liberation, we never forgot to add that special sentence to the traditional words of the ancient Hagadah.

"Grandmother, what happened after you left the village? Did you go back to visit the Tokolys again? And when did you come to Israel?" Omer asked.

"We tried to repay the Tokoly family, those noble souls, as much as we were able. After the war there was chaos in Europe for a long time. Trains didn't run—except for military needs and other essential reasons—and cars had no fuel or spare parts. There was a shortage of food and of the day-to-day necessities. The stores were empty. Basic foods were available only with special ration coupons. The black market flourished and people were hungry for bread. Many cities had suffered heavy damage and the infrastructure was destroyed. Still, the people in the villages got along pretty well when it came to food, because they all raised animals and grew fruits and vegetables. But other items, such as kitchen utensils, clothing, medicines, and so forth, were scarce for everyone.

"When we visited the Tokolys, we brought with us everything we managed to get hold of in the city. I remember one visit when we brought them thread, which was worth a lot at the time and could be bartered for other goods. And when

my parents returned to their old professions and began to earn a living, even if it was barely enough to scrape by, we brought them a little money, too. We stayed in constant and close touch with them, visiting one another in the village and the city. When our economic situation improved, Mother and Father supported them regularly and we became inseparable, sharing in each other's happy and sad times alike. When Anna's younger brother became ill with tuberculosis, for example, we visited him frequently in the hospital; but unfortunately he died, and we went to the funeral. We stayed in close touch until we came to Israel in 1947, two years after our liberation."

"Grandmother, can you tell me now about how you came to Israel and all the stories about your first years here?" Omer asked. "Promise me you'll tell me the rest of the story, grandmother!"

"I promise that if I have the strength to start writing again, I will do that for you. But how I came to Israel and started a new life here is a story in itself."

Epilogue

After we came to Mandatory Palestine, in 1947, we stayed in touch with the Tokoly family from the village of Jarok. However, our correspondence tapered off somewhat, because of our difficulties of integration and the War of Independence, which broke out soon after our arrival. Mother and Father lived in a tent in a new immigrants' camp for about a year. The little money they managed to bring with them ran out quickly; their economic situation was dire and they barely earned a living. We girls were sent to institutions of the Youth Aliyah (immigration) organization.

We continued to correspond with Anna and Vincent until Slovakia was taken over by the Communists. In 1949, when the Iron Curtain cut off Eastern Europe, we lost touch with them completely. By indirect means, we learned that Anna had given birth to another son, but two years later we were shocked to hear that the young mother had died of tuberculosis — she was only 30. We mourned her for years, just like a member of the family. The forced separation that was caused by world politics and the Cold War did not extinguish our admiration and love for them.

Fifteen years later, Mother fell ill with a terminal disease and died; Father died a few years after her. The three daughters raised families, studied, worked and entered into the routine of life. But all those years, we waited for the day when we would be able to be reunited with "our peasants" and revisit, this time as free human beings, the "pit" that was our home and haven for seven months.

After the fall of the Communist regimes in Eastern Europe, we took the first opportunity—the three sisters and our husbands—and went back to the village. We didn't find "our pits," because the peasants had filled them in and sealed them, planting a vineyard there, as in days long past. We were sorry that we couldn't show our husbands our underground home or photograph it for the grandchildren.

I think I could write a whole book about the emotional meeting we had with Ela, the daughter of Vincent and Anna, who already had a family of her own. She remembered our names and said they had all been concerned about us over the years, because of all the wars in Israel. She too had longed to meet us. We were terribly sorry to hear that her father, too, whose handsome features reflected his beautiful soul, had died many years before, still a young man. He had taken to drinking in order to drown his sorrow at Anna's loss and died of alcohol poisoning.

Our visit took place on a summer Sunday. We all went to the local cemetery, which was filled with visitors, and paid our last respects at the graves of the noble, wonderful couple. The others looked at us curiously, though some of them knew about us from stories they had heard.

As we walked back through the streets of the village, we

were thrilled when some of the churchgoers who were on their way home recognized us and began reminiscing about those long ago times, filling us in about details we didn't know. One aged man of about 90 told us he used to send Moritz (as Father was known) bread and cheese with Vincent. As we strolled through the village, all the memories of those last days of the war came rushing back vividly.

We also visited other places that had been landmarks on our many escapes. It was important for us to see that small, narrow opening to the street in the basement of the building from which we had escaped. Deeply moved, we stood on the sidewalk, this time in the light of a clear day, in front of the window. As we recalled those intense moments of our daring escape, the whole scene seemed to replay itself. We measured the width of the opening and we couldn't believe that 13 people had escaped through it on that Christmas Eve.

The street was busy and many of the passersby must have wondered about this group of people who spoke a foreign language and were bending over to measure the width of the window using their hands. None of them could have guessed what a drama had occurred here decades earlier, in those bleak, black times.

In Michalovce, my place of birth, we were very disappointed at being unable to find even a trace of the old Jewish homes. The magnificent synagogue had also vanished as though it had never existed. The authorities had erased every sign of the Jewish community that had existed here for hundreds of years. We came to the hospital where I was operated on in order to secure our release, but did not enter: I had no desire to go inside again.

Back in Israel, we met with the directors of Yad Vashem, told them our story and made an official request for the commemoration of the wonderful couple who, without asking anything in return, had supported and comforted us in those days of horror that we suffered at the hands of inhuman criminals. We were convinced that Vincent and Anna deserved to be recognized as Righteous Among the Nations, and our request was granted. That special couple was awarded the Certificate of Honor of the Jewish People, even if they themselves, unfortunately, were not privileged to receive it. Ela, their daughter, accepted the certificate — a token of appreciation for her parents' humanitarian deeds — at a solemn ceremony held at the Israeli Embassy in the capital of Slovakia. We hosted Ela and her husband in Israel in 1991, and we continue to write to one another and to visit.

It's said that the apple does not fall far from the tree. In the Gulf War, when we were deeply anxious about a possible gas attack — and the word "gas" has a harsh connotation for most Holocaust survivors — we received a warm invitation from Ela and her family to stay with them until the war ended. "As my parents helped you survive in those hard times, I too want to give you shelter and protection against the missiles that are liable to fall on you."

I wrote back that our situation was nothing like it was back then. Now we had a state and an army to protect us, this is our country and we would not seek shelter anywhere else. At the same time, their concern, attention, and devotion had touched us deeply and we were grateful for their offer. We would never forget her parents. I took my children to Jarok, too, so they could see the place for themselves and meet the family from which had come two of the very few people who had considered it a divine commandment and obligation to help others, despite the danger to themselves. I hope that our grandchildren will also remember the story of our amazing journey to survival, which had a happy end thanks in great measure to those wonderful people, Anna and Vincent Tokoly.